Neglect in the North of Ireland

Neglect in the North of Ireland

Odrán de Bhaldraithe

Ebb

Ebb Books
Unit 241
266 Banbury Road
Oxford, OX2 7DL

© 2023 Ebb Books

The right of Odrán de Bhaldraithe to be identified as author of this work has been asserted by them in accordance with sections 77 and 78 of the Copyright, Designs and Patents Act 1988.

Paperback ISBN: 9781739985271
Ebook ISBN: 9781739985288

*British Library Cataloguing-in-Publication Data*
A catalogue record for this book is available from the British library.

Typeset in Dante
ebb-books.com

*Do na glúintí romham, a throid nuair a bhí orthu troid: Saoirbhreathach agus Pádraig Mac Craith, Séamus agus Breandán Ó Doibhlin, agus Séamus Ó Siridéáin.*

## Contents

*A Note on Terminology*   3

*A Further Note on Framework*   5

1. Introduction: A State Trapped in Its Own Existence   7
2. Economic Neglect: A Society That Is Not Its Own   15
3. Political Neglect: What Power? What Sharing?   39
4. Cultural Neglect: No Moon   80
5. Conclusion: Revolutionary Neglect   98

# A Note on Terminology

While some of a leftist persuasion might consider it "quixotic" to refuse to use the imperial nomenclature imposed on our home in order to make it appear to be outside the Irish nation, I count myself among those who will not use the official title of the six-county state in the North of Ireland. Where the official title of the Northern state is used in someone else's speech or writing, or in the name of an organisation, I will not change that. Those previously unfamiliar might wonder how a name can be so contested. The answer is to be found in the writings of Paul Stewart, Tommy McKearney, Gearóid Ó Machail, Patricia Campbell and Brian Garvey: "What kind of society cannot call itself by a commonly agreed name? A society that is not its own, perhaps?"[1]

Similarly, political groups can all too often be split into too many or too few categorisations due to the one dominant

---

[1] Paul Stewart, Tommy McKearney, Gearóid Ó Machail, Patricia Campbell, and Brian Garvey. 2018. *The State of Northern Ireland and the Democratic Deficit: Between Sectarianism and Neoliberalism*. Glasgow: Vagabond Voices, p. 33.

polarity in Northern politics. Catholics, nationalists and republicans are often conflated; I will use republicans to refer to those who once did, or still do, hold revolutionary aims and were once, or still are, associated with physical force republicanism, such as Sinn Féin (in its Provisional, Official and Republican offshoots) and the Irish Republican Socialist Party. The terms Protestant, unionist, and loyalist are often also used interchangeably; I will use unionist to refer to anyone who favours the continuation of Britain's colonial presence in Ireland and makes that a central part of their political project.

# A Further Note on Framework

This essay takes as its framework colonial analysis and the analysis that the current form of the Northern state is the continuation of British colonial rule in Ireland, which is best elucidated by Robbie McVeigh and Bill Rolston in *Anois ar theacht an tSamhraidh: Ireland, Colonialism and the Unfinished Revolution*. Some disagree with this analysis out of wilful ignorance, for ideological reasons, or for more reasonable reasons. The historian Brendan O'Leary, whose work on the North remains stellar, falls into the latter category, but this does not make him any less wrong than, say, the unionist blogger and ideologue Jamie Bryson. McVeigh and Rolston disagree[1] with his assertion that the Good Friday Agreement represents the "final decolonisation" of Ireland;[2] their work proves as much to be true. Hopefully, the study that follows

---

1    Robbie McVeigh and Bill Rolston. 2021. *Anois ar theacht an tSamhraidh: Ireland, Colonialism and the Unfinished Revolution*. Belfast: Beyond the Pale, p. 8.
2    Brendan O'Leary. 2019. *A treatise on Northern Ireland, Volume I: Colonialism*. Oxford: Oxford University Press, p. 131.

of Britain's continued economic, political and cultural domination of the North does the same.

## 1. Introduction: A State Trapped in Its Own Existence

April 2023 marked 25 years since the signing of the Good Friday Agreement and the official end to the war that has come to be euphemistically known as "the Troubles", its name obscuring the fact that the latest in a series of revolutionary offensives against the British presence in Ireland was being waged. It is now 102 years since the partition of Ireland was formalised by Britain and the Northern state was created to maintain Britain's hold in what was, at the time, Ireland's industrial heartland.

2023 finds the North confronting challenges it was designed to never encounter: the biggest party in its Assembly is Sinn Féin, the party that was once the political wing of the Provisional IRA, the largest republican paramilitary during the latest round of Ireland's struggle for independence, whose entire *raison d'être* is nominally the destruction of the Northern state. The 2021 Census of the North showed a population of 1.9 million people, bringing Ireland's total population to seven million and, for the first time in the short history of the North, showing there to be more people of a Catholic background than a Protestant one.[1] While it has always been simplistic to think of the conflict in the North as a religious one rather than a colonial one, the history of the conflict has unfolded in such a manner that has made it an unavoidable truth that the majority of those who favour reunification are Catholics and that the majority of those who favour the continuation of the British presence in Ireland are Protestants. The British presence in Ireland has long been explicitly sectarian upon religious lines, which is of course fitting given that it is a colonial presence of a state whose head is the leader of the Protestant faith. As Frank Kitson, the British Army's head in Belfast from 1970-72 and ur-philosopher in fighting guerrilla insurgencies, wrote: "It may be of interest to recall that when the regular army was first raised in the seventeenth century, 'Suppression of the Irish' was coupled with 'Defence of the Protestant Religion' as one of the two main reasons for its existence."[2] Look no further than the eventual leader of Ulster unionism that rose through the stage of the conflict that Kitson participated in, the Free Presbyterian preacher Ian Paisley, to know that things had not progressed for the better in this regard. It has been easy for

---

1   Rory Carroll. 22 September 2022. "Catholics outnumber Protestants in Northern Ireland for first time." *The Guardian*.

2   Frank Kitson. 1971. *Low Intensity Operations: Subversion, Insurgency, Peace-keeping*. London: Faber and Faber, p. 24.

lazy commentators to thus simply imagine Irish opposition to colonialism as a reactionary counter-offensive mounted on behalf of the majority faith held in the country, Catholicism. The opposite has in fact often been the case, with the Catholic clergy, barring some notable exceptions, often fervently anti-republican. When the Anglo-Irish Treaty signed at the end of the Irish War of Independence codified the partition of Ireland, those who chose to fight on for the republican cause of all of Ireland in the Irish Civil War were told they would be, and in some cases were, excommunicated.

The Northern state was, in keeping with the British colonial project in Ireland, designed to be a Protestant state with a Protestant parliament, as its first Prime Minister and founding father James Craig said. The presence of Sinn Féin at the top of that parliament and a majority of Catholics within the boundaries of that state, specifically designed to ensure a Protestant majority in perpetuity, is thus notable and inevitably raises the question of the state's future. To understand the North's future, or possible lack thereof, we must, of course, understand its past. This is best done in three distinct stages: the rule of the one-party, proto-Fascist Orange State (1921-1972) wherein the civil service, government, corporations, secret societies such as the Orange Order and the Royal Black Institute, and the armed wing of the state (the Royal Ulster Constabulary, the B-Specials and later, the Ulster Defence Regiment) combined in order to crush the designated other of the Northern state, the Catholic people largely of a republican outlook, via unemployment, low-wage work, oppression of cultural expression, and sporadic pogroms; direct rule from London during 'the Troubles' (1972-1998); and the 'peace process' (1998-present), during which power has been shared under the terms of the Good Friday Agreement.

The present moment is one of various crises – economic, identitarian, governmental – for the North: Catholics are in the majority and a republican party is the largest in the Assembly; the economy faces a new global recession having never recovered its levels of production from before the 2008 recession; hospital waiting lists are at all-time highs while health spend is, contradictorily, at an all-time high; the cost of living crisis seen elsewhere is biting hard; suicide rates remain high, higher than in England, the South, or Wales, and people from the lowest income areas are twice as likely to commit suicide as those in the highest income areas;[3] wages are low and the proportion of the population deemed economically inactive remains disproportionately high; and the constituent Assembly, Stormont, remains inactive months after the May 2022 election. The Democratic Unionist Party, the party of Paisley and the largest within unionism, refuse to return to

---

3   Maurice Fitzmaurice. 26 May 2022. "Northern Ireland suicide figures review results in 'downward revision' of numbers." [online] *Belfast Live*. Available at: https://www.belfastlive.co.uk/news/northern-ireland/northern-ireland-suicide-figures-review-24066946 [Accessed 4 October 2022].

their seats due to their opposition to the Protocol on Ireland/Northern Ireland, the mechanism agreed between the European Union and the British Government to allow the North unfettered access to both the British and EU markets post-Brexit.

As such, the North finds itself in a confusing position. Unionists are refusing to return to the state institutions, the very bodies that administer the partition that is the fulcrum of their political ideology, while republicans beseech them to return and make Stormont work. This is, of course, a reversal of roles from the previous period of inactivity for Stormont from 2017 to 2020, when Sinn Féin collapsed the Assembly due to then-First Minister Arlene Foster's refusal to temporarily step aside while an investigation into her role in the Renewable Heat Incentive scandal was carried out and subsequently refused to return once that investigation was completed unless a raft of minor reforms, largely based around cultural demands such as legislative protection for the Irish language, were agreed. Three years on from the assurances they had been given under the *New Decade, New Approach* document that led to Sinn Féin returning once again to the institutions, *Acht na Gaeilge* – the colloquial name given to what is now the Identity and Language (Northern Ireland) Act – has been passed by Westminster following unionist refusal to legislate for it after the Assembly had returned. Whether or not it will now be implemented within the North's political system, or left to wither on the vine like abortion access has since it was also passed by Westminster, will depend on the return of Stormont. With Sinn Féin the largest party in the North and the joint-largest in the South, and widely tipped to lead the next Dublin government, they scramble to resurrect Stormont and show that they can govern in the sensible neoliberal mode favoured in the halls of power on both sides of the border. They find themselves unable to prove their authority due to the crisis facing unionism, however.

Having signed up to the Brexit project as a last gasp attempt at remounting a hard border in Ireland, unionism finds itself spurned by the British and facing the reality that what they consider their mainland does not consider them at all. The Conservative Party in England had no qualms in signing up to the Protocol because it achieved what Brexit had aimed for: Britain out of the European Union. That it did not bring the North with it was of no concern to them or to those in Britain who supported Brexit. In fact, polling shows that those who voted leave would rather have lost Britain's hold on the North than to have stayed in the EU.[4] Facing this reality, screaming into a void about how the Protocol violates their rights as British citizens, violates the Good Friday Agreement, and violates the North's place in the so-

---

4   Michael Ashcroft. 19 June 2018. "Leave Voters Would Rather Lose Northern Ireland Than Give Up the Benefits of Brexit". *The Telegraph*.

called United Kingdom, unionists find themselves sometimes indulged by anti-EU tough talk from the Conservatives but never getting what they want in the form of the scrapping of the Protocol. Unable to get what they want, they have simply gone limp, refusing to budge or participate in the institutions that administer the British rule that they hold so dear.

The Good Friday Agreement made this an inevitability, formalising Northern politics into a system whereby two competing ideologies simultaneously shared power and raced towards opposing end games. In Brexit, unionism saw its opportunity to override the Agreement and rid themselves of the possibility of a future border poll. Sinn Féin on the other hand seek to ride the wave of the increasing Catholic population, their growing popularity in the South, and anti-Brexit reaction on both sides of the border towards a border poll and the reunification of Ireland. Polling now shows that two thirds of voters want a border poll in the wake of Brexit, but 49% in the same poll stated that they would vote to remain under British rule.[5] The problem with both of these approaches is that they are constituted within the framework of Good Friday Agreement governance. The Agreement was the latest political treaty to enshrine Britain's stranglehold over Irish affairs, meaning that nobody in the

---

5   Michael Savage, and Lisa O'Carroll. 29 August 2021. "Majority of Northern Irish Voters Want Vote on Staying in UK". *The Guardian*. https://www.theguardian.com/politics/2021/aug/29/majority-of-northern-irish-voters-want-vote-on-staying-in-uk.

North can either scrap the Protocol or convene a border poll. Such decisions remain the sole domain of the British. Neither can anyone in the administration of the Northern state affect the crippling economic conditions to any real degree given that all public funding is provided by Britain on a block grant basis. The North is once again stuck at a crisis point, unable to change, a state trapped in its own existence.

This essay seeks to analyse neglect in the North of Ireland in all its guises: economic, political, and cultural. It seeks to interrogate what is neglect and what is not and who is guilty of neglect and who is not in the colonial context of Britain's continued rule in this part of Ireland. There are some who would use the information that will follow as a means to argue for the more efficient, more democratic administration of the Northern state, and that Northern society should be allowed to become its own. This essay will not. It will identify the root cause of this neglect as the root cause of all malfunction in the North: continued British rule. It is only by unifying with the South and destroying the idea of an exclusively Northern society that the people of the North can escape this deep-seated decay and create a society that is entirely its own.

## 2. Economic Neglect: A Society That Is Not Its Own

To understand the ruination of the Northern economy and the neglect by a seemingly permanent austerity, we must first understand how Northern public funds are generated. The Assembly retains little power over taxation, and thus revenue raising. In the rare case where Stormont is in charge of a tax – the air passenger duty long-haul flight tax, for example – the Sinn Féin-DUP duopoly has moved to act in the interest of business. Having gained control of the long-haul flight tax in 2012, Stormont immediately scrapped it. The Corporation Tax (Northern Ireland) Bill, passed by Westminster and the House of Lords in March 2015, allows the Executive – the body atop the Assembly comprising power sharing ministers – to set the corporation tax for the North, again something that both Sinn Féin and the DUP pledged to use to act in the interest of businesses by reducing it from 21% (at the time, now 19%) to 12.5% in order to match the criminally low rate in the South – a tax haven according to multiple academics, including James R. Hines Jr.,[1] and a 2019 European Parliament vote recommending that it and other "EU tax havens" be added to the European Commission's list of tax havens. Despite the pledges of the leading parties of both sides of the power sharing agreement in the North at the time, this power has never been exercised and as such, the North's corporation tax remains the same as Britain's. Along with the power to raise some regional rates, this is the extent of the North's power to organise its own finances.

Unable to even borrow from other bodies, such as the EU when it had been a member, the North is thus entirely reliant on the block grant that it receives annually from the Westminster government. While the amount received from the block grant had previously been subject to rumour and rounded figures with no clarity, in 2021 the British Government published its Block Grant Transparency Report, accounting for the amounts provided to the devolved assemblies in Scotland, Wales, and the North of Ireland every year. According to the report, the North has received figures ranging from £9.885 billion to £14.884 billion during the years 2016/17 to 2020/21[2] for day-to-day spending (known in the report as RDEL) and an extra £1.042 billion to £1.627 billion in so-called long-term funding, designed to fund long-term infrastructural

---

[1] James R. Hines Jr. 2010. "Treasure Islands". *Journal of Economic Perspectives*. p. 103-125.

[2] HM Treasury. 15 December 2021. *Block Grant Transparency Report*. London.

investments such as hospitals, roads, etc. The amount that the North of Ireland – as well as Scotland and Wales – receives is determined by the Barnett formula, developed and first used by the former chief secretary to the British Treasury, Joel Barnett. The formula calculates the amounts given to each devolved administration by using the previous year's budget as its baseline and calculating increases via the amounts afforded to public spending increases per capita in England and then dividing them based on the percentage of the given area's population relative to England's. Under the new Northern population of 1.9 million, as stemming from the 2021 Census, this means that the North would be owed 3.4% of the spending increases per capita in England, as 1.9 million is 3.4% of England's population of 55.98 million. The amount arrived at by the Barnett formula can of course be topped up via political agreements, as was seen following the 2017 general election in Britain, when the DUP agreed to a confidence and supply agreement with Theresa May's government in return for further funding.

The block grant has long been criticised as insufficient and unable to meet the needs of a Northern economy that has been creaking with neglect for so long that multiple key sectors require sustained investment into the billions of pounds to even function. While the totals given in the block grant can sound large, it must be taken into account that aside from paying for public expenditure on sectors such as healthcare, education, and housing, the £14.884 billion figure is also used to pay public and British armed forces pensions, and account for the North's share of British military spending, royal family costs, British national debt, and, in days gone by, the EU subvention. What this leaves is a situation where annual increases in public spending are often negligent, if not outright negative, in real terms. Upon the British government's publication of the projected block grant totals to 2024/25, the Stormont Finance Minister, Sinn Féin's Conor Murphy stated that the apparent increase for 2021/22 was not an increase in real terms and predicted day-to-day spending rises of £450 million in 2022-23, £670 million in 2023-24, and £866 million in 2024-25,[3] increases that will almost certainly be devoured by the rapid inflation seen in the economy since the publication of those figures.

What this almost total British control over finances in the North has created is a situation that can be, at best, described as neglect, a neglect that is perhaps at its clearest in the North's ailing, disgraceful health system. Of the total projected final spend of £13.001 billion in the North's 2021/22 budget, the health sector accounted for £6.451 billion, almost half of the total budget. Recent research by the Northern Ireland Fiscal Council predicts per annum increases in health spending of 2.3-3%, meaning that the level of health spend could eventually account for as much as 77% of current block

---

3   John Simpson. 10 January 2022. "The Budget: Frustrated Financial Ambitions on the Hill". *Belfast Telegraph*.

grant totals.[4] While an outsized focus on health in any budget in that period is understandable due to Covid-19, what the North's 2021/22 budget did was simply continue a trend of attempting to plug a hole that is many years deep. Years of neglect prior to Covid and following the British policy of contracting NHS services[5] out to private providers have created a system where receiving routine medical care can take multiple years and even situations where lives are in danger are not given due attention. The Ulster Unionist Party (UUP) Minister for Health Robin Swann set a 2021/22 draft target for cancer care services of 95% of patients urgently referred with suspected cancer beginning their treatment within 62 days. Figures compiled by the Northern Ireland Statistics and Research Agency (NISRA) show that the target has not been met on a regional level for three years and the gap that exists shows no realistic sign of being bridged any time soon. In March 2022, just 48.1% of those urgently referred by their GP with a suspected cancer had begun definitive treatment within 62 days,[6] an annual fall from the 49.2% that had begun their treatment within 62 days in March 2021, meaning that the service has actually regressed with the lifting of Covid

---

4   Northern Ireland Fiscal Council. 27 September 2022, *Sustainability Report 2022: Special focus – Health*. Belfast.
5   The North is not actually part of the NHS but its equivalent organisation, Health and Social Care (HSC), is in every way equivalent, down to its ruination.
6   David Whelan. September/October 2022. "The state of ill-health". *AgendaNi*. Issue 110, p. 8-11.

restrictions. Of the five health boards that make up the Northern HSC, not one has reached the target of 95% since the western board did so in April 2017. From the March 2022 figures, only two boards – south eastern and western – treated more people within the target time than outside of it, recording figures of 52.4 and 51.6% respectively.

Emergency services are not faring any better. Department of Health figures released in July 2022 show that 7% of emergency department attendees left before their treatment had been completed, a 75% increase in proportion from the roughly 4% average recorded in 2014. Department of Health targets for emergency care are that 95% of patients attending type 1, 2, or 3 emergency departments be treated, discharged, or admitted within four hours of arrival and that no patient should be waiting longer than 12 hours. June 2022 saw 51.5% of patients seen within the four-hour timeframe, a 7.5% fall from the same month in 2021. An extra 2,704 patients were also found to have waited over the 12-hour target when compared with 2021, with a total of 8,192 patients waiting over 12 hours. This increase in the proportion of those waiting over 12 hours occurred despite the fact that emergency departments had experienced an almost 5% drop in attendances. Compared to the 51.5% of people seen within the targeted four hours, 12.9% were forced to wait beyond 12 hours, a wait that is targeted to never occur.

The situation is somehow worse for day-to-day healthcare.

The Department of Health's targets state that 50% of patients should be waiting no longer than nine weeks for a first outpatient appointment and that no patient should be waiting longer than 52 weeks. By the end of June 2022, 80% of patients were waiting longer than nine weeks and over half were waiting more than 52 weeks, meaning that it was significantly more likely that a patient would be waiting more than a year for their first outpatient appointment than to have their first appointment within the targeted time.

Another one of the Department of Health's aims is that no more than 55% of patients are left to wait longer than 13 weeks for inpatient or day case treatment, with the ultimate target of no patient waiting longer than 52 weeks. Again, the latest figures show a total failure in this regard, with the number of patients waiting to be admitted to hospitals rising by 10% over the year June 2021-June 2022. More than 80% of patients were waiting longer than 13 weeks to be admitted. Over 58% were waiting longer than 52 weeks.

Diagnostic targets are also being missed out on. By March 2022, the targets set were that 75% of patients should be waiting no longer than nine weeks for a test and nobody should be waiting over 26 weeks. 52.6% of patients were waiting over nine weeks for a diagnostic test by the end of 2022, and 27.1% were waiting more than 26 weeks.[7]

---

7   Northern Ireland Statistics and Research Agency. 25 August 2022. *Northern Ireland waiting time statistics: diagnostic waiting times*. Belfast.

The health service is often held up as an example of what could be lost upon the unification of Ireland, that the loss of a free-at-the-point-of-service health system would turn people away from the idea of a united Ireland. These figures show that the people who mount this argument are either acting in bad faith or availing of private healthcare, totally unfamiliar with public on-the-ground healthcare in the North of Ireland. The reality for the average person in the Northern state is that healthcare is free at the point of service, yes, but the odds of actually receiving that service in anything approaching a timely manner are not in their favour.

Other basic infrastructure fares no better. The housing stock in the North has increased to over 814,000 homes over the past 20 years, but the pace of growth within the sector was decimated by the 2008 financial crash and has never shown any signs of recovery. Having held an annual rate of 11,500 new homes per year pre-2008, the annual growth rate now stands at 6,400 homes per year, just above half of the pre-crash rate. The 6,446 new dwelling completions in 2020/21 represented a 12% decrease in completions from the amount recorded in 2019/20, though of course these figures do come with the caveat of Covid-19 restrictions in place at the time restricting construction activity. The amount of new dwelling starts within 2020/21 also showed a 9% decrease on 2019/20.[8]

---

8   Department for Communities. 9 December 2021. *Northern Ireland Housing Statistics 2020-21*. Belfast.

The stats provided by the Department for Communities also show that the housing supply in the North is at the mercy of the private sector, with private construction accounting for 89.3% of all new dwelling starts and 89.9% of all new dwelling completions in 2020/21.

This occurred despite the fact that the North's social housing waiting lists are recording record amounts of people: 43,971 applicants were on the social housing waiting list as of March 2021, with 30,288 of those deemed to be in "housing stress", a classification that is arrived at via questionnaires in the application regarding the applicant's current living situation. To reach 30 points and thus be defined as being under "housing stress", an applicant is accepted to be living in unsafe or unsuitable accommodation. Of the households on the social housing waiting list, 9,889 are accepted as statutorily homeless. While this status has often confused unfamiliar satellite commentators, it does not mean that 9,889 households were living on the streets of the North during 2020/21; it does, however, mean that 9,889 households were either living in temporary or emergency accommodation or living in unsuitable accommodation. A homelessness bulletin published in March 2022 and covering the second half of the year 2021, found there to be 3,596 households living in temporary accommodation[9] – a figure that rose in the first

---

9   Department for Communities, Northern Ireland Statistics and Research Agency, and the Housing Executive. 10 March 2022. *Northern Ireland Homelessness Bulletin, July-December 2021*. Belfast.

half of 2022 to 3,658.[10] In terms of actual rough sleeping, this was found to have been on the rise before Covid and the extended provision of emergency accommodation that arose because of it. The Housing Executive's last rough sleeper count was performed in November 2020 and it showed that the total numbers of rough sleepers had halved across the North, down from 36 in 2019 to 18 in 2020. 38 had been recorded in 2018.[11]

These record numbers regarding homelessness, housing stress, and basic housing need take place against a glacial-paced social housing building programme. In the period 2010/11-2020/21, the number of annual social housing construction starts under the Social Housing Development Plan (SHDP) reached 2,000 or over just three times; the number of completions never reached 2,000, and only reached 1,500 or over four times. At the current rate of building, it is estimated that it will take over 50 years to clear the North's housing waiting lists.[12] This lack of supply has of course translated into a price squeeze in the private market. While the North's housing prices remain very low when compared to the South, where property prices are among the

---

10   Department for Communities, Northern Ireland Statistics and Research Agency, and the Housing Executive. 15 September 2022. *Northern Ireland Homelessness Bulletin, January-June 2022*. Belfast.

11   The Housing Executive. 2020. *2020 Rough Sleeping Count/Estimates*. Belfast.

12   Andrew Madden. 23 August 2022. "Concern As Northern Ireland's Social Housing Waiting List Could Take 50 Years to Clear". *Belfast Telegraph*.

most pertinent of issues to have powered the Sinn Féin rise there, and compared to Britain, the North's house price index for quarter three of 2022 stood at 158.8 when using quarter one of 2015 as 100, showing a 4.1% quarterly increase and a 10.7% yearly increase. The average price for a house now stands at £176,131.[13]

The neglect in the North's housing and health sectors tell similar stories: unable to borrow money in order to bring the Northern state into the 21st century, local politicians are left to stretch scraps given to them by the British that can never do anything more than paper over cracks that are entirely made by the lack of funding delivered by the British in the first place. Of course, this lack of funding is no oversight on the part of the British, but this is a point that will be returned to in this essay's conclusion. Such is the level of neglect the tight purse strings of the British have caused in the North that it is quite literally impossible to answer the housing demand. A 2021 report by the Utility Regulator recommended an investment of over £2 billion pounds in the wastewater system in the North,[14] which had been degraded and underfunded to such a degree that it meant that over 100 areas within the Northern state were at their developmental capacity. Similarly, a 2019 report by the Northern Ireland Audit Office found that the

---

13   Northern Ireland Statistics and Research Agency. 16 November 2022. *NI House Price Index, Quarter 3 2022*. Belfast.

14   Rebecca Black. 6 July 2021. "Addressing water infrastructure issues could take 12 years, Infrastructure Minister Nichola Mallon says". *The Irish News*.

road network in the North needed an investment of £1.2 billion for maintenance after years of neglect.[15] Consider the annual increases in day-to-day spending as predicted by Finance Minister Conor Murphy – £450 million in 2022-23, £670 million in 2023-24, and £866 million in 2024-25 – along with the emergency situation in health that requires almost half of the annual budget be spent addressing shortcomings that actively kill people and it is impossible to see how the North solves these issues while dependent on the largesse of the British Government.

Another core public sector left underfunded and neglected is education where, before the collapse of the Assembly, officials from the Department of Education were telling Stormont's Education Committee that the education budget, second only to health in overall terms, was "wholly insufficient".[16] An example of the neglect that is caused by the underfunding and subsequent need to focus all funding on health was seen in the plans that Murphy was developing in his draft three-year Executive Budget, which was to be Stormont's first multi-year budget in years. The draft budget was published without cross-party approval and thus was always likely to change, had it progressed to such a stage, but it contained within it a prioritising of increasing health

---

15  Northern Ireland Audit Office. 26 March 2019. *Structural Maintenance of the Road Network*. Belfast.
16  September/October 2022. "Education budget 'wholly insufficient'". *AgendaNi*. Issue 110, p. 68-69.

spending, leading to a 2% cut in most other departments. An increase in the block grant meant that the Department of Education then avoided these cuts and was to receive £2.431 billion in 2022/23, £2.471 billion in 2023/24, and £2.503 billion in 2024/25. The multi-year budget, however, never progressed to the stage where it could be agreed and implemented, falling victim to the Assembly's collapse in the aftermath of Sinn Féin's victory at the polls in May 2022.

During the preparation for this draft budget, the Department of Education submitted its resources bids to the Department of Finance, as every department must do. Education assumed a baseline resource department expenditure limit of £2.270 billion for the year 2022/23 and also factored in pressures which were deemed to be either inescapable or pre-committed, such as those arising from Covid-19, various education programmes and the *New Decade, New Approach* agreement, and found that they would have a funding gap of £366.1 million in 2022/23 if the estimated funding figures were delivered. This gap would then increase to £450.7 million in 2023/24 and £543.5 million in 2024/25. The Education Committee had previously identified four areas that would be particularly affected by any funding gap: Covid-19 safety and resourcing (a concern that will have undoubtedly abated by now), special education needs provision, resources to ensure the emotional and mental wellbeing of children such as access to the outdoors and early interventions, and equal opportunities. Demand for special education needs is now outstripping the amount of places available in the North: as of 5 July 2022, there were a total of 103 students with a statement of special education needs who were without a place for the current academic year, 2022/23. Department of Education figures show that 57,833 pupils with special education needs are being educated in mainstream schools, 55,128 of whom have no specialist provision within their schools.[17] The neglect of these children by the educational sector is reflected in the fact that children with a special education needs statement make up 6.3% of the pupil population, but 15% of home-schooled pupils known to the Education Authority possess a statement, reflecting a trend of parents turning away from a system that long ago turned away from their children.

This utter neglect and depression of a public sector and any sort of welfare security net then conspires with the private sector to create a society where "poverty is fundamentally central to this economy: poor jobs, poor housing and poor democratic representation are inextricably bound together".[18] The North's economy is like something of a bad joke. While it may have initially been boosted by what is known as the "peace dividend", an onrushing of outside and domestic

---

[17] September/October 2022. "SEN demand outstripping places". *AgendaNi*. Issue 110, p. 80-81.
[18] Stewart et al., p. 52.

investment in the wake of the Good Friday Agreement giving businesses the green light, telling them that it was safe to invest in the North once more, productivity and investment shot up, as they did elsewhere during a period of over speculation that would come to a crashing halt in 2008. What occurred in the North has been described as a "double transition" by the economist Conor McCabe: a transition to peace from a time of war, and a transition to the norms of the neoliberal economy that had been cementing itself elsewhere, not least in the South, while the North had been at war. "Modern investors do not see exceptions in the world, only opportunities," McCabe writes.

Eastern Europe, South Africa and Northern Ireland are all unique in terms of the dynamics of their history and geography. What they have in common is that they found themselves as societies in transition at a time when economic thought had solidified around neoliberal principles. This 'double transition' – towards peace and neoliberalism – has been mediated through the world of finance, law, accountancy and politics. It is the financialisation of the economy that demands low pay and privatised services, not geography, history or conflict. And financialisation is the key aspect of the neoliberal turn.[19]

---

19  Conor McCabe. 2012. *The Double transition – The Economic and Political Transition of Peace*. Belfast: Irish Congress of Trade Unions.

Stewart, McKearney, Ó Machail, Campbell, and Garvey add to this understanding of the peace process Northern economy while offering their own progression of the idea: that the North's economy contains within it one variant from Britain's neoliberalism: "declining manufacturing replaced by even less rooted capital in the service economy, typically represented by the sector emblematic of the new economy, the transient call centre".[20]

A 2015 report by the Trade Union Congress found that the "struggle for a decent day's work in return for decent pay and conditions has intensified",[21] and this struggle has only continued through the intervening seven years, the Covid crisis and the looming global recession. NISRA's Annual Survey of Hours and Earnings found that median gross weekly earnings for full-time employees in April 2021 were £575, an increase of 8.8% from £529 in 2020. This was the largest annual increase of weekly earnings on record, a stat caveated by the fact that it had been immediately preceded by the largest annual decrease on record, 1.1% in the year to April 2020. Real weekly earnings increased by 7%, again the largest annual increase on record, but again immediately following on from a steep decrease of 2.0% the year beforehand. While these figures may spark cause for optimism among those who

---

20  Stewart et al, p. 16.
21  The Trade Union Congress Commission on Vulnerable Employment. 2015. *The Decent Jobs Deficit: The Human Cost of Zero-Hours Working in the UK.*

would seek to defend the North, both its economy and its ruination by Britain, in comparison with the British economy the people of the North are suffering in relation to supposed equals. Weekly earnings in the UK stood at £611, an increase of 4.3% from 2020 (£586) and real UK weekly earnings increased by 2.6% over the year. Median annual earnings in the North increased by 1.7% for full-time employees to £29,000, a full £2,000 lower than the UK median of £31,000.[22] The Asda Income Tracker found the North of Ireland to have had a bigger contraction in discretionary income than any region in Britain on an annual basis in quarter two 2022, recording a decrease of 28.7% from Q2 2021, compared to a total drop in the tracker – encompassing Britain and the North of Ireland – of 14.1%. This has left households here with just £95.14 of weekly discretionary income, compared to a UK average of £209.15.[23]

The work of the economist Paul MacFlynn of the Nevin Economic Research Institute (NERI) shows that, by the middle of the 2010s, "the growth in annually managed expenditure, which mostly consists of social transfers, halted its growth and flatlined in the years after".[24] While the economic crash of 2008 sparked austerity across Europe, economies elsewhere

---

22  Northern Ireland Statistics and Research Agency. 26 October 2021. *Annual Survey of Hours and Earnings*. Belfast.

23  Asda Income Tracker. October 2022. London: Centre for Economics and Business Research.

24  Paul MacFlynn. 18 November 2021. *Incomes in Northern Ireland – A decade of change*. Belfast: Nevin Economic Research Institute.

had begun to move on and, gradually, increase spending per capita and governmental borrowing as interest rates reached zero. This was obviously not the case in the North, where borrowing is impossible and a seemingly permanent austerity was guaranteed by the block grant, which delivered meagre real increases if it delivered real increases at all. Meagre rises were also seen in the period 2010-2020 in average gross household income, which started in 2010 at just below £800 (using 2020 prices) in 2010, before cratering through the decade below £700 and then slowly recovering to a level of above £800 in 2020. House prices, by contrast, have risen in the North by over 50% since 2015, a time when wages have not remained static but have just barely increased.

On a macroeconomic level, the North has never recovered from the 2008 crash. The Northern Ireland Composite Economic Index, an index compiled by NISRA measuring the economic output of the North, has never returned to its peak of 2007. Using both 2009 and 2019 levels as 100, the index has only been recorded at 100 or over in 2006, 2007, 2008, 2009, 2019 and 2021 during the period 2006 to 2021. Having recorded a high of 104.9 in quarter two of 2007, quarter two of 2022 showed a score of 104.7,[25] but with another recession coming, this long and painful attempt at recovery will fall

---

25    Northern Ireland Statistics and Research Agency. 29 September 2022. *NI Composite Economic Index Statistical Bulletin, Quarter 2 2022*. Belfast.

short. With no control over its own finances, recession in Britain means recession for the North. The nail was driven into this coffin when the Bank of England announced that it would raise its interest rates as it attempted to combat a predicted 13% inflation rate by year-end 2022. Danske Bank Consumer Confidence Indices carried out in the North found that the rate of people who expected their financial position to worsen rose from 26% in quarter four of 2021, to 40% in quarter one 2022, and then again to over 50% in quarter two 2022. Ulster Bank's monthly survey of the private sector reported falls in construction and retail activity in May 2022, and as these sectors are cornerstones of the Northern economy it is clear that the recovery is over.

The North has a productivity gap of 17% below the average of the United Kingdom, a fact made all the more galling when it is remembered that the British economy's productivity has been largely stagnant since the 2008 economic crash.[26] This lack of productivity comes despite record numbers of employment in the North: May 2022 saw the North's labour market record 779,000 people in employment, a record high, and the unemployment rate was 2.6%, just above the pre-pandemic record low of 2.3%. Economic inactivity – a grouping which includes students, those in retirement, disabled people and those with long-term illness – has long been a problem for the North and has been

---

26  September/October 2022. "Protocol provides short-term boost but recession looms". *AgendaNi*. Issue 110, p. 36-39.

recorded at a rate consistently above 40% in the population aged over 16 between 2017 and 2022. In comparison, the rate in Britain has been recorded consistently at just above 35%.[27] Given that the gap in these levels was prevalent before Covid, and exacerbated thereafter, the North's recent history of conflict coupled with its inability to provide a functioning healthcare service play a large role in this gap. Average hours worked have also taken a beating recently; while the hours of part-time workers remain the same when compared to pre-pandemic levels, the average hours of full-time workers have dropped from 33.9 in 2019 to 32.8 in April 2022.

The Protocol remains the biggest issue at the heart of mainstream economic discussion in the North. Designed to keep the British-imposed border in Ireland as invisible and open as possible, it allows the North access to both the EU single market and the British internal market. Research by the London School of Economics and the Resolution Foundation found that in a Brexit scenario where the Protocol is retained, which unionists are currently campaigning against, refusing the return to the Assembly until it is scrapped, the North's economy would be less affected than the economies in Britain. With the Protocol in place, the North's economy would still suffer damage, with output falling by 0.7% (compared to 1.1% without the Protocol), but this would be

---

27  Paul MacFlynn. September/October 2022. "Where have all the workers gone?". *AgendaNi*. Issue 110, p. 44-45.

less than the UK average fall in output of 1.3%.[28] Brexit has already changed the Northern economy: the 2021 Northern Ireland Economic Trade Statistics report published by NISRA showed record growth from 2020-2021, the first year of the Protocol's operation, in total sales (13.6%), internal sales within the Northern state (13.2%), and sales to the Republic (23%). Sales to Britain (13.1%) and the rest of the EU (16.8%) also experienced double figure percentage point growth,[29] showing the unionist claim that the Protocol limits capitalist trade to any area to be a blatant lie. By June 2022, the Central Statistics Office, the official statistical collator of the Republic, was reporting that Northern sales to the South over the first six months of 2022 had increased by 21% when compared to the first six months of 2021,[30] just after the Protocol had come into effect in January 2021. The balance of the North's economy, especially its external sales, is totally different to that of the South and its exports. Given its status as a tax haven that is the European headquarters of some of the largest technology firms, the South's exports are majority services rather than goods by a margin of 52% to 48%. The North's external sales are goods by a vast majority, which makes sense

---

28  Swati Dhingra, Emily Fry, Sophie Hale, and Ningyuan Jia. June 2022. *The Big Brexit: An assessment of the scale of change to come from Brexit*. London: London School of Economics Centre for Economic Performance and the Resolution Foundation.

29  Northern Ireland Statistics and Research Agency. 14 December 2022. Northern Ireland Economic Trade Statistics. Belfast.

30  Central Statistics Office. *Goods Exports and Imports June 2022*. Dublin.

given the importance of agriculture to the economy – 1.6% of gross value added, as compared to 0.9% in the UK and 0.5% in the South, with a total gross output of £2.43 billion in 2021[31] and accounting for 66% of Northern sales to the Republic in 2015-2016[32] – and the rump of manufacturing that is still left; goods account for 82% of external sales, with services making up the other 18%.[33]

However, those singing the praises of the Protocol, including republicans and the so-called constitutionally neutral parties such as the Alliance Party, should be wary. The North's function for Britain reveals what it is: a colony. Under total financial control of Britain, it receives enough to ensure that people do not starve to death and little else. It presents British business with a desperate low-wage English-speaking workforce to which it can offshore its services, allowing the presence of the North, now only sweetened by its access to the European market, to play a disciplining role on British workers and allowing British wages to be depressed – proving Marx's evergreen statement that for British workers "the national emancipation of Ireland is not a question of abstract justice or humanitarian sentiment but the first condition of

---

31  Northern Ireland Statistics and Research Agency. 30 June 2022. *Statistical Review of Northern Ireland Agriculture 2021*. Belfast.

32  Northern Ireland Statistics and Research Agency and the Department for the Economy. 21 June 2018. *Cross-Border Supply Chain Report*. Belfast.

33  Martina Lawless. December 2021. *Cross-border Trade in Services*. Dublin: Economic and Social Research Institute.

their own social emancipation".[34] It would appear that those who argue the virtues of the Protocol do so from the position that it would benefit the North to open cheap English-language labour to Europe as well as to Britain, leveraging the access to both markets the North has as nobody else does. With this approach, the two options will be to follow the Southern model and expand the role of service exports from multinationals that see Belfast as a cheap market both in terms of real estate and salaries, giving them a foothold in both markets and evolving the next step of McCabe's double transition, or alternatively doubling down on the Northern state's dominant agriculture sector and increasing trade with both the South and the rest of the EU. Either approach ends with the North in a similar situation to the South: at the beck and call of foreign direct investment, forced to depress wages and slash taxes (if the North is ever given control of them) in order to satiate the appetites of the never satisfied FDI. Given that those who support the Protocol are also those who have signalled their intentions in the past to lower the corporation tax rate, it should come with no doubt that this is the intention.

The problem with the North is that it is not its own society and can never become its own while the Northern state exists. What ensures that the North is not its own is its

---

34   Karl Marx. 9 April 1870. "Marx to Sigfrid Meyer and August Vogt in New York" from *Selected Correspondence*. Progress Publishers, 1975, p. 220-224.

status as the last remnant of the British colonial project in Ireland and the economic domination that Britain ensures within the North creates the alienation from our own power. Stewart, McKearney, Ó Machail, Campbell, and Garvey are also correct to use the example of a call centre, as this is in effect what the North is for Britain, an offshore tract of land wherein people who speak English trade goods and services back to the so-called mainland; the North thereby functions as something of a call centre for Britain. That the people tasked with leading the charge for the end of the societal alienation from power in the North – namely, republicans – are at the forefront of a campaign designed to simply extend the North's status as call centre to the European mainland should worry anyone invested in true Irish freedom, but sadly would not come as a surprise to anyone attuned to how power in the North has functioned in the peace process era.

## 3. Political Neglect: What Power? What Sharing?

The Protocol is an ostensibly unionist mechanism. Like Scotland but unlike Wales and England, the North voted to remain in the European Union in the 2016 Brexit vote, with a total of 56% in favour of retention of EU membership. Unlike Scotland, the North is not in Britain and borders an EU member state – the Republic – from which 614,252 people in the North hold a passport,[1] making them citizens. The Protocol was thus designed to solve the contradictions of Britain's presence in Ireland as highlighted by Brexit: by technically coming out of the EU single market but retaining access to it and simultaneously remaining in the British market, the North's status as both bordering a member state and as a constituent state of the UK was to be respected.

What is required to support the Protocol on the terms on which it was implemented is recognition and legitimation

---

1   Northern Ireland Statistics and Research Agency. 22 September 2022. *Census 2021 main statistics demography tables – passports held*. Belfast.

of the partition of Ireland, something that would have been anathema to previous generations of republicans, but is now deemed common sense by Sinn Féin in the peace process era. Recognition and legitimation of partition within Sinn Féin is a process that was begun long ago and was codified upon the passage of the Good Friday Agreement in 1998. Chief among the victories of the agreement touted by Sinn Féin was the provision that stated that British Secretary of State for the North would call a border poll "if at any time it appears likely to him that a majority of those voting would express a wish that Northern Ireland should cease to be part of the United Kingdom and form part of a united Ireland". The problem with this, for republicans at least, is that the agreement also states that in this scenario, reunification would be carried out

> by agreement between the two parts respectively and without external impediment, to exercise their right of self-determination on the basis of consent, freely and concurrently given, North and South, to bring about a united Ireland, if that is their wish, accepting that this right must be achieved and exercised with and subject to the agreement and consent of a majority of the people of Northern Ireland.[2]

At least, this arrangement – that two separate votes would take

---

2  Northern Ireland Office. 1998. *The agreement: Agreement reached in the multi-party negotiations.* Belfast, section 1, clause ii.

place in Ireland regarding unification, one in the South and one in the North – had once been a problem for republicans. The farcical 1973 border poll posed a simple question to the people of the North: would they prefer membership of the United Kingdom, or to join with the Republic for a united Ireland? The option to retain the union passed with a vote share of 98.9% because republicans had boycotted, claiming that a vote regarding Irish unification that took place in just six of Ireland's 32 counties was a denial of Irish self-determination, a partitionist mechanism via which partition could not be solved.

"Democracy is the central concept of republicanism," Liam Ó Ruairc writes. "It holds that the people of Ireland have the right to self-determination as a unit without external impediment – all-Ireland democracy. It rejects the British state's interference in Irish affairs as a barrier to democracy and views this as the root cause of the conflict in Ireland."[3] Sinn Féin abandoned this traditional republican position when they signed the Good Friday Agreement, which recognises the "legitimacy of whatever choice is freely exercised by a majority of the people of Northern Ireland with regard to its status, whether they prefer to continue to support the Union with Great Britain or a sovereign united Ireland". The agreement takes for granted another position that was anathema to republicanism pre-1998, the idea of the

---

3   Liam Ó Ruairc. 2019. *Peace or Pacification? Northern Ireland After the Defeat of the IRA.* Winchester: Zero Books, p. 48.

Northern people as separate from the South, the codification of the partition not just of the Irish body politic but of the Irish nation itself. Long gone is the idea of the founding father of Irish republicanism Theobald Wolfe Tone that the nation could "substitute the common name of Irishman in place of the denominations of Protestant, Catholic, and Dissenter [a contemporaneous term for Presbyterians]"; now Sinn Féin speaks of a future united Ireland where the "British" identity of Protestants in the North, some of whom are descended from the Scots that planted Ulster in the 17th century, would be "protected and respected",[4] abandoning Wolfe Tone's hope of uniting the nation and fully integrating the planters as the Anglo Normans had been before them – implicitly recognising the British imperialist construct that modern Northern unionists, born and raised in Ireland largely to parents and grandparents born and raised in Ireland, are somehow British. By signing an agreement that affirms its adherents will "recognise the birthright of all the people of Northern Ireland to identify themselves and be accepted as Irish or British", Sinn Féin can no longer claim the legacy of Wolfe Tone or his republican ideals.

What is at play in the peace process era is the culmination of the slow stripping away of traditional republican ideals that was first signalled when Sinn Féin voted at its 1986 *ard*

---

4   Jonathan Rainey. 21 April 2017. "A united Ireland would 'protect and respect' British identity". *The Impartial Reporter.*

*fheis*[5] to put an end to its policy of abstaining from the Dáil in Dublin. The argument had, until that point, been that to enter the 26-county parliament in Dublin was as bad as entering the six-county Assembly in the North and the UK Parliament in Westminster; either one was as much a recognition and legitimation of partition as the other. The motion to cease the boycott of the Dublin institutions was passed in 1986, but the party *ard fheis* is remembered by those critical of the reformist slant Sinn Féin increasingly took on due to a legendary speech given by Ruairí Ó Brádaigh, one-time president of Sinn Féin and abstentionist Teachta Dála from 1957-1961.

Ó Brádaigh, who split with Sinn Féin after the decision to end abstentionism and went on to found Republican Sinn Féin, told the *ard fheis*: "Once you accept the institutions of the state ... you will not be able to do it according to your rules, you have to do it according to their rules." Following their entrance into the Southern institutions in 1986, Sinn Féin's entrance into the Northern institutions became inevitable. After the Good Friday Agreement in 1998, they only accelerated their willingness to act in accordance with the parliamentary rules of so-called liberal democracies. The party has now taken on the social mores of any vaguely left-of-centre party in Europe; having previously been committed Eurosceptics from the inception of the European project,

---

5   The term for a national conference used by many of Ireland's political parties.

Brexit has seen them reverse their attitude and preach unity as a means of returning the North to the EU. They reassure big business that they will not target them in government,[6] they no longer vote against the Southern Irish state's retention of the non-jury Special Criminal Court – created to imprison Provisional IRA members and decried as a human rights violation by Amnesty International and the UN – and they now apologise time and time again for revolutionary republican actions or for the legitimate expression of republican goals and opinions, as they did when party President Mary Lou McDonald apologised for the IRA's assassination of Lord Mountbatten, when Brian Stanley apologised for his tweet praising the IRA's operation on the Narrow Water that killed 18 British soldiers, and again when McDonald apologised for standing behind a banner in a New York City parade that carried on it the most basic of republican demands: England get out of Ireland.

Nobody can make the argument that the Sinn Féin approach has not been successful for Sinn Féin. The 2020 general election in the South saw the party win the joint most amount of seats with Fianna Fáil, with 37[7] seats, and it recorded the highest

---

6   Hugh O'Connell. 10 October 2021. "Pearse Doherty Interview: 'Big business and investors know Sinn Féin won't go after them'". *Irish Independent*.

7   Although technically Fianna Fáil hold 38 seats, one of these was automatically returned as it belongs to reigning Dáil Ceann Comhairle Seán Ó Fearghaíl.

percentage of first preference votes, 24.5%. This upturn in fortunes saw the party gain 15 seats in the Dáil and saw a swing of 10.7% in their vote share. Scrambling, the establishment parties of Fianna Fáil and Fine Gael, traditionally associated with opposing sides in the Irish Civil War that followed the signing of the Anglo-Irish Treaty in 1921, but whose politics have become largely inseparable during the liberalisation of the Southern economy, were forced into an official coalition together for the first time along with the Green Party. The time since the election has only been kind to Sinn Féin, as the tri-party coalition has failed to solve the South's record numbers of homelessness, rising house prices and now an energy crisis caused in part by a willingness to open the State to any electricity-guzzling data centre open to the possibility.

The story of the 2022 Assembly election in the North was a similarly triumphant one for the party: Sinn Féin received 29% of the first preference vote, smashing its nearest rivals in the Democratic Unionist Party, who recorded a first preference rate of 21.3%. This result reflected Sinn Féin's near-total monopolisation of the parliamentarian sphere of republicanism/nationalism, with the SDLP – their nearest rivals in this case, as representatives of the middle class Catholic reactionary establishment and doyens of the peace process – recorded a vote share of just 9.1%. In total votes too, Sinn Féin dominated – recording over 250,000 first preference votes when no other party even approached 200,000. Yet Sinn

Féin only have two more seats than the DUP in the 90-seat Assembly and 10 more than the Alliance, the next biggest party. Despite their vote share increasing, they did not in fact increase their number of seats, although the story of the election was certainly one of a triumphant Sinn Féin.

The success for the party has come at a price, and that price has been the total neglect of the progression of republican thought by the ideology's largest party. If anything, given the numerous climb downs, the ideology can be said to have curdled in the peace process era. Where the Troubles saw republican prisoners of war spend their time in internment camps dedicating themselves to learning the Irish language endangered by British colonialism,[8] or reading Mao to develop new military strategies for the next stage of the fight,[9] Irish republicans now attend conferences in Dublin's 3Arena for €7.10 a ticket to be regaled of stories about the "new and agreed Ireland" by actors such as Colm Meaney and James Nesbitt, along with Southern politicians like Leo Varadkar, telling a crowd that – upon reunification – the North could retain its own health service, police service and the Stormont Assembly. The fact that he was "jeered"[10] by the crowd when

---

8   Feargal Mac Ionnrachtaigh. *Language, Resistance and Revival: Republican Prisoners and the Irish Language in the North of Ireland*. London: Pluto Press.

9   Richard English. 26 April 2012. *Armed Struggle: A History of the IRA*. London: Pan, p. 254.

10   John Manley. 3 October 2022. "Leo Varadkar cautions against securing united Ireland by slim majority". *The Irish News*.

suggesting this hints that there may still be some hope.

It was republican principles that catapulted Sinn Féin to their status as the largest republican party, in a scene that was once heavily populated by the Irish Republican Socialist Party and Official Sinn Féin[11] and others. "Sitting in Leinster House is not a revolutionary activity," Ó Brádaigh told the 1986 *ard fheis*, and the same is doubly true of sitting in Stormont. The strategic objective of the peace process, Anthony McIntyre wrote, was to "include republicans while excluding republicanism",[12] or, as leader of the Ulster Unionist Party David Trimble put it, to put "an end to violence" and ensure "a commitment to exclusively peaceful and democratic means",[13] thereby re-establishing the Northern state's monopoly on violence and forcing republicans to function within the rules of the British system in the North. It is a familiar path, the one Sinn Féin have been treading since 1998. Fianna Fáil and the anti-Treaty IRA followed it after they arose from the decision to retain abstentionism as a policy at the 1926 Sinn Féin *ard fheis*; James Connolly's Labour Party and the Irish Citizen Army did similar following the establishment of the Irish Free State six years after Connolly's execution for his part in the 1916 Easter Rising; and the Official IRA

---

11   Later Sinn Féin the Workers' Party and later again simply the Workers' Party.

12   Anthony McIntyre. 12 April 1998. "Why Stormont Reminded Me of *Animal Farm*". *Sunday Tribune*.

13   David Trimble. 25 October 2007. "Ulster's lesson for the Middle East: Don't indulge extremists".

and Official Sinn Féin that split from what is now known as Sinn Féin eventually did the same, taking a more winding path through Soviet Union-inspired Marxist-Leninism before arriving at outright reformism and counter-revolutionary positions. All three parties now populate vast swathes of the Southern establishment. The historian Brian Hanley, who wrote the definitive guide to Official republicanism, is fond of quoting former Official IRA chief of staff Cathal Goulding, saying: "We were right too early, [Gerry] Adams was right too late, and Ruairí Ó Brádaigh will never be fuckin' right."[14] A funny quote, but it is Ó Brádaigh who has been proved right: having accepted the institutions of both states in Ireland, Sinn Féin now play by their rules, like the Officials, Labour and Fianna Fáil before them. Even before partition, when radicals pushed for full Irish independence in the early 20th century but reformists called for Home Rule and a devolved Dublin parliament within the United Kingdom of Britain and Ireland, this willingness to play within the British-enforced rules was prevalent. "Home Rule ... is now but a cloak for the designs of the middle class desirous of making terms with the imperial government it pretends to dislike," Connolly wrote. "It is but capitalist liberalism with an Irish accent. As such, it is the enemy of every effort of working class emancipation."[15]

---

14  Brian Hanley and Scott Millar. 29 April 2010. *The Lost Revolution: The Story of the Official IRA and the Workers' Party*. Dublin: Penguin, p. 596.

15  James Connolly. 8 July 1899. "Socialism and political reformers". *Workers' Republic*.

This has never been more clear as it has been in the fallout from Britain's vote to leave the European Union. Despite decades of committed Euroscepticism on the part of republicans, Sinn Féin took the decision to support the remain campaign in the North, wishing to draw another distinction between themselves and the unionists supporting Brexit. Having viewed republicanism as revolutionary for decades, they saw an opportunity to portray republicanism as a credible ruling ideology within the EU – ready to take their sensible politics continent-wide. Brexit was largely decried in Ireland as reckless, and it would have been reckless had it not been so considered on the part of unionism. The supposedly unthinkable outcome of a hard border was exactly what the Democratic Unionist Party desired, to drive as permanent a wedge as possible between the North and the South. Against this gamble, Sinn Féin sought to cast itself as the steady hand of grown-up politics and in doing so further donned the skin of limp, uninspiring, constitutional nationalism of the SDLP that Sinn Féin themselves had killed as an electoral force. Sinn Féin had already begun on their path towards the neoliberal centre, with the closure of hospitals by their Stormont Minister for Health, Social Services, and Public Safety Bairbre de Brún and the use of public-private partnerships by Martin McGuinness when he was Stormont Minister for Education – but in Brexit they saw their opportunity to fully take the leap, to close the circle that the Good Friday Agreement had started to trace.

The core of the Sinn Féin argument regarding Brexit was correct: the British call for sovereignty as expressed through their vote to leave the European Union highlighted the contradiction of Britain's denial of Irish sovereignty, but this is a denial of sovereignty that Sinn Féin signed up to in 1998. The Protocol's impasse leaves the British with three choices: recognise the truth of Marx's words that denying Irish sovereignty limits their ability to exercise their own and withdraw from Ireland, double down their support for unionism and strike for a hard border, or climb down from their opposition to the Protocol and convince the unionists to do the same because it is an ostensibly unionist mechanism that allows the continuation of the union, grants Britain its leave from the EU, and smooths over the contradictions of their occupation of Ireland that the Brexit vote highlighted. The latter is the most likely.

The 2022 Assembly election has seen the continuation of the recasting of political roles in the North that Brexit began. Unionists refuse to return to Stormont while Sinn Féin are begging them to do so. The republicans are now arguing for the restoration of the institutions of Irish partition in order for them to function smoothly; the neglect of the republican ideology has become degradation.

Ó Brádaigh's is the road not taken for Sinn Féin. The Éire Nua policy, first published in 1971 and later updated to include details of its proposed federal system, was the brainchild of Ó Brádaigh, his brother Seán, and Daithí Ó Conaill – Ó Brádaigh's vice president in both Sinn Féin and republican Sinn Féin. The policy called for a united Ireland governed by a three-tiered system: federal, provincial, and local, with a "federal parliament of approximately 15 deputies, half would be elected directly and the other half would be sent forward in equal numbers from the provincial parliaments".[16] These reforms to governance structures would be backed up by "a new constitution and charter of rights for a united Ireland"[17] and "an updated social and economic program".[18] Influenced by both Ireland's ancient Brehon laws, in which land and property were communally owned, the *Conhar na gComharasan* philosophy that envisioned the establishment of co-operatives, and the African socialism of Julius Nyerere[19], Éire Nua was a decidedly Irish solution that was in dialogue with the greater anticolonial movement worldwide. As Ó Brádaigh himself understood, the policy placed the republican movement as "spiritually, at least, part of a worldwide movement to increase the dignity of man now threatened with being submerged by the consumer society".[20]

---

16   Robert W. White. 2020. *Ruairí Ó Brádaigh: The life and politics of an Irish revolutionary*. Bloomington: Indiana University Press, p. 187.
17   Ibid.
18   Ibid.
19   Ibid., p. 165.
20   Ibid., p. 194.

The structures proposed under Éire Nua would be bottom-up, starting with community councils "based on parishes or other suitable centres",[21] through to district councils consisting of "a single chamber elected by the people of a clearly defined area",[22] to regional boards feeding into provincial parliaments or assemblies governing the four provinces of Ireland, and finishing with the federal parliament at the top. Ó Brádaigh envisioned the Irish people "acting as a unit"[23] through these proposals, with the localised nature of power within the system designed, in part, to ensure unionists could "maintain their identity and some political power".[24] The structures would also give Ireland the chance to arrest its uneven development – tilted totally towards Belfast in the North and Dublin in the South – and grow its regions in a balanced manner through collectivised farming, nationalisation of industries such as commercial banking and mining, and the establishment of worker-owned co-ops in industries such as manufacturing, agriculture, and fishing.[25]

While the importance of some of the above industries have been crushed by Ireland's entrance into the European project, the principles of the policy – the end of Britain's colonial presence in Ireland, the localisation of power, and

---

21 Republican Sinn Féin. *Éire Nua: A federal democratic socialist republic.* Dublin: Republican Sinn Féin, p. 26.
22 Ibid., p. 25.
23 White, p. 188.
24 Ibid., p. 268.
25 Ibid., p. 165.

the introduction of democracy into the workplace – remain sound and its current version echoes Ó Brádaigh's recognition of Ireland's international responsibilities as it calls for an Irish withdrawal from the EU in order to situate a new Irish state among the other former colonies of Europe:

> We can best serve the interests of our own people and of humankind by maintaining a principled non-aligned stance in international affairs, avoiding military alliances and promoting the cancellation of Third World debt. Our democratic and egalitarian principles and our own long struggle for national independence should lead us to promote human rights and the liberation of people everywhere.[26]

In Ó Brádaigh's time, federalism was also seen by unionists as the most acceptable of outcomes should a united Ireland happen. Upon meeting for the taping of a 1974 episode of the TV show *Weekend World*, Ó Brádaigh and Ulster Defence Association press officer Sammy Smyth agreed that a federal Ireland could lead to a "permanent peace".[27] During the period of Éire Nua being Sinn Féin's flagship proposals for the future of Ireland, it was estimated that the creation of Dáil Uladh – the provincial parliament for Ulster that would govern the entirety of the province's nine counties rather just the six of

---

26 Éire Nua, p. 14.
27 White, p. 214.

the North – would have a working majority of unionists, but this is no longer the case given the electoral and population shifts best seen in the May 2022 election and the 2021 census. Unionist domination under an Éire Nua type system would now likely begin at the regional board level, namely the East Ulster board under the Ulster provincial assembly, and bleed down to the community council level in several areas.

That there are regional disparities within both states in Ireland that any united Ireland should look to remedy is in no doubt. CSO data for 2019 showed that only five of the South's 26 counties – Dublin, Kildare, Cork, Limerick, and Wicklow – have average disposable income per person rates above the state's average,[28] showing an average-distorting concentration of wealth in the east through Dublin, Kildare, and Wicklow, and the urban centres of Limerick and Cork. The Northern state retains such regional disparity within a much smaller land mass: gross disposable income per head across the 11 district council areas reaches as high as £19,795 in Lisburn and Castlereagh, and as low as £15,470 in Derry City and Strabane.[29] The type of federalism envisioned under Éire Nua would almost certainly guarantee the combatting of such uneven development in Ireland, but criticism of the plan and its eventual abandonment by Sinn Féin centred instead

---

28  Central Statistics Office. 16 February 2022. *County Incomes and Regional GDP*. Dublin: Central Statistics Office.

29  Office for National Statistics. 13 October 2022. *Regional gross disposable household income, UK: 1997-2020*.

on it being a "sop to unionism".[30] The idea that "unionists" would need to be protected in a united Ireland gives credence to the lie that unionism is an identity, rather than the political ideology based on material domination that it is. Unionism cannot be accommodated in a system that guarantees a political structure "without any group infringing on the rights of others"[31] because infringing on the rights of others in order to guarantee hegemony is precisely what unionism is predicated upon. The achievement of a united Ireland of any nature, federal or not, requires not just the necessary defeat of unionism as an ideology but the incorporation of at least some of its former adherents into the new united state; in the case of the socialist republic envisioned by Connolly and Éire Nua, this would be the working class. Under the terms of a British withdrawal necessary for the achievement of a united Ireland, unionists would no longer have a unionist political project to which they could wed themselves and would have to become something entirely new. Their majority Protestantism and cultural mores would of course not be under attack, and any truly socialist project would surely incorporate them via material means, rendering their incorporation on the basis of their being unionists moot. If not, it would fall to those designing such plans to answer the question of what safeguards would be in place to prevent the wrecking of a bottom-up governmental structure by

---

30   White, p. 274.
31   Éire Nua, p. 3.

community councils and regional boards opposed to the political project.

These are the issues that anyone looking to formulate a republican future vision for Ireland must wrestle with, but the underlying principles of Éire Nua remain sound. At the very least, they must be a springboard for creating a compelling alternative from the bourgeois consensus politics of events such as Ireland's Future. While republican groups such as Republican Sinn Féin and Cumann na mBan still adhere to the Éire Nua vision, it cannot be said that these ideas have any purchase in the mainstream political imagination today. It is said that once Roy Johnston and Seán Ó Brádaigh had drafted the original Éire Nua, it was then the Ó Brádaigh brothers and Ó Conaill who "took it down from the shelf"[32] and formulated Éire Nua I and II. It is time for those standing outside the Sinn Féin consensus in republicanism to come together and take these ideas of old down from the shelf of obscurity and begin once again with the process of creating a vision for what Ireland would look like after reunification beyond vague paeans to the socialist republic.

In colonised countries, radical politics are typically accounted for by the twin planks of national liberation movements and trade union movements; if republicanism has curdled into degradation, the same can be said of the trade union

---

32   White, p. 165.

movement in the North. The trade union movement here is plagued by a "mindset that rejects any and every form of radical action that might possibly discomfort the local devolved administration in Stormont."[33] Unions have suffered because they too have fallen victim to the suffocating nature of the Good Friday Agreement and the Overton window that came with it in the North, whereby those who are critical of the arrangements made under the aegis of the peace process are "thus hostile to 'peace' and support going back to armed conflict".[34] Their hesitance to step outside of the agreed narrative of the peace process and advocate on behalf of its members was perhaps best summed up by Peter Bunting, then secretary general of the Irish Congress of Trade Unions, when he told *The Irish News* that the ICTU had performed a U-turn on the 2015 Fresh Start agreement because "we looked into an abyss and we withdrew from the abyss because the inevitability of having a major opposition campaign against our own politicians was catastrophic in the long term for us".[35]

Playing little to no role in promoting an understanding of the denial of Irish democracy and self-determination that is the partition of the country, the trade union movement instead plays the basic role of celebrating jobs regardless of their context, hamstrung by the typical union arrangements

---

33 Stewart et al, p. 151.
34 Ó Ruairc, p. 147.
35 Stewart et al, p. 151.

of British and Irish workers being together in a single union. This was perhaps at its most evident when Steve Turner, the London-based assistant general secretary of Unite the Union and one-time candidate for general secretary, repeatedly stated his support for the continued manufacturing of Royal Air Force fighter jets by Spirit AeroSystems in Belfast, at one point using the hashtag #BuildItInBritain without a hint of irony. What Turner showed by signalling his support for the continued manufacture of war machines in British-occupied Belfast for use in Britain's 21$^{st}$ century imperial wars was the lack of a broader mindset within trade union circles. As long as people are getting paid, it does not matter that they are serving their colonial master's continued decimation of the global working class in places like Iraq and Afghanistan. That various Irish leftist organisations, such as the Communist Party of Ireland, came out in support of Turner during his campaign for general secretary shows that this problem is not a British-specific one, but one that has spread to the Irish understanding, or rather the lack thereof, of how British colonialism functions in Ireland today.

Similarly, Stewart et al, while correct overall in their diagnosis of the issues with the trade union movement in the North, misdiagnose the issues on two key points. Firstly, they state that a cessation of the kowtowing to Stormont as seen in Bunting's quotation is necessary to "overcome the sectarian curse by providing a strong class-based alternative (or genuine opposition) to the sterile venal structure that is Stormont Mark II",[36] but this ignores that, central to the idea of workers' power, is an enlarged franchise whereby democracy and self-determination are extended to the workers who are the majority of any nation. This is an impossibility within the Stormont system because its existence, and the existence of the Northern state, "constitutes a denial of the self-determination of the majority"[37] of Ireland. Secondly, they remark that "some of our labour movement leaders imagine it is clever to be involved in what is in effect a dubious, and in any case superficial, partnership agenda, when what they are actually helping to deepen by their participation ... is privatisation of our public services".[38] What is ignored here is the financial set up of the Northern state itself. The cynical nature of the British block grant is what guarantees the privatisation of public services within the Northern state; it is delivered at such a low level precisely in order to guarantee such an outcome as it is the preferred outcome of the British government. The game is rigged anywhere but it is doubly rigged in the North. It is necessary for the trade union movement to realise that the only coherent way to argue for the cessation of privatisation, for the extension of the franchise to allow workers to meaningfully participate in democracy and self-determination, and the end of the

---

36  Stewart et al, p. 161.
37  Ó Ruairc, p. 46.
38  Stewart et al, p. 162.

"sectarian curse" that the Good Friday Agreement codified into the structures of government, is to argue for the end of the North's existence and the reunification of Ireland into one democratic structure – just as it did in the movement's heyday in Ireland at the beginning of the 20th century when it was led by James Connolly and Jim Larkin. In Connolly's conception of politics, "the first act of the workers will be through their economic organisations seizing the organised industries; the last act the conquest of political power".[39] Instead, what has happened is that organised labour has admitted defeat in its challenging of the political arena by any meaningful definition and allowed itself to be swallowed by political power –limiting its effectiveness due to its acceptance of the superficial partnership agenda that seeks to obscure the necessary demarcations of opposing political positions. Lenin wrote that the "spontaneous development of the working class movement leads to its becoming subordinated to the bourgeois ideology",[40] and that is seen in the North through such mimicry.

There is a need here to remind both the unions and Sinn Féin of Connolly's words, that the struggle for control of the capitalist state – more so the occupying capitalist statelet – is only the "echo of the battle",[41] and that the true battle will

---

39  James Connolly. April 1908. "Sinn Féin and the Language Movement". *The Harp*.

40  Vladimir Ilyich Lenin. 1983. *What Is to be Done?* Moscow: Progress Publishers, p. 48.

41  Connolly, Sinn Féin and the Language Movement.

be fought over economic interests. It is thus in the interests of republicans to organise unions and to "raise the level of consciousness of the workers generally",[42] on the basis of fighting for a united Ireland and the creation of a labour force that recognises the truth of Connolly's maxim of the cause of labour being the cause of Ireland and vice versa. Whether such moves are done within existing unions or new ones would be the choice of those executing such plans. While this organising would undoubtedly be decried as sectarian by those within the labour movement who value incremental wage increases over true conditions of workers power, the term sectarian has been bludgeoned into meaningless by its overuse in the North. It is not sectarian to organise via the political lines by which the situation in Ireland is to be understood unless one argues that it is politically sectarian, but such a complaint is easily dismissed as necessary in a colonial struggle.

A unionist may or may not think favourably upon the wage demands of certain workers, but – as a unionist – they believe in the locating of power within six counties of Ireland outside of Ireland, meaning that their ideology is not commensurate with the ultimate goal of workers' power and democracy. There seems to be little to no appetite for understanding that a member of the working class can be actualised as a political subject through unionism rather than

---

42   Lenin, p. 48.

through trade unionism, and this almost childlike treatment of working class unionists must be reckoned with if the labour movement in Ireland is to move past these juvenile positions. Trade unionism as it exists in the North today favours "remaining intact at the expense of any radical action",[43] and this is a position that must be attacked through republicanism, Ireland's radical tradition. With public services failing and the political institutions immobilised in the North, there will never be a more opportune to assemble a critical core of workers capable of the type of strikes that would render the Northern state unworkable.

Republicanism ignores labour at its own peril, as Liam Mellows discovered during the Irish revolution. Writing to Austin Stack from Mountjoy Jail, where he was to be executed in 1922, he stressed: "We should certainly keep Irish labour for the Republic: it will be possibly the biggest factor on our side. Anything that will prevent Irish labour becoming imperialist and 'respectable' will help the Republic."[44] The actions he prescribes echo Lenin's decrying of spontaneous development; the failure of the republicans to fully synthesise republicanism and labour in his time ended in the tragedy of his execution along with three other comrades and the cementing of partition and two counterrevolutionary states in Ireland. To repeat this mistake again in the drive to unify

---

43  Stewart et al., p. 150-151.
44  C. Desmond Greaves. 2004. *Liam Mellows and the Irish Revolution*. 2nd edition. Belfast: Foilseacháin an Ghlór Gafa, p. 364.

Ireland would be a farce, as both Sinn Féin and the labour movement in the North are doing.

It is fitting that Stewart et al would refer to this partnership agenda codified by the Good Friday Agreement as superficial. The partnership of republicanism and unionism must remain superficial in order to maintain the Northern institutions that it propagates, and so, hand in hand with the neglect of radical politics in the forms of republicanism and trade unionism, comes a neglect in the understanding of the unionist ideology with which republicans have partnered. This neglect comes, of course, because to tell the truth about unionism would give it an image that would make it unacceptable for even the most moderate of movements to partner with it.

In his consideration of the foundation of the Orange Order in Armagh in 1795, wherein lies the genesis of the organisation of modern-day political unionism, the English Marxist historian T.A. Jackson wrote:

> Under a pretext of zeal for law, order, and the Protestant religion an oath-bound secret society on the Masonic model was organised, which, in practice, proved a fomenting centre, as well as a cloak of protection, for the organised knavery into which the Peep-of-Day Boys had degenerated. The Orange Order became an organised conspiracy of all the most degenerate reactionaries of every social strata – an instrument whereby the lumpen

strata were used as tools to break up the solidarity engendered by the United Irishmen, and to replace the struggle for democratic advance by disintegrating it into an embittered war of sect against sect, from which the only ones to profit were the Clare-Beresford clique in Dublin Castle and their hangers-on of every social grade.

In evaluating the Orange Society it must not be forgotten that the bodies it was founded to disrupt and destroy – the United Irishmen and the Defenders – functioned, the one as a great liberating force, and the other as a tenants' protection league and an agrarian trade union. The Orange lodges functioned as a "union-smashing" force, operating in the interest of an oligarchical clique threatened with overthrow by a revolutionary-democratic advance. They constituted the first Fascist body known in history.[45]

Little has changed with regard to unionism. It is still a political ideology and movement that has as its *raison d'être* the denial of Irish self-determination and democracy, which manifests itself through various guises, chief among them anti-worker policies and attitudes and a continuation of the cultural mores of the planters from which many unionists are descended – a sneering contempt for anything native to Ireland, such as

---

[45] T.A. Jackson. 1947. *Ireland Her Own: An Outline History of the Irish Struggle for National Freedom and Independence.* 3rd ed. London: Lawrence and Wishart, p. 145.

the Irish language, Irish traditional music, Irish sports as constituted within the Gaelic Athletic Association, and of course, Irish self-determination. When unionism was given its day in the sun by the British upon the 1921 partition of Ireland and was able to found the Northern state via Article 12 of the Anglo-Irish Treaty, "it was clear what it [the state] was not: 'not-Catholic', 'not-Irish', 'not-Gaelic', 'not-native'".[46] Like any Fascist movement worth its salt, the unionists had their designated other, the constant alien threat that would have to be subdued.

By the time the Northern state was founded, its social construction was already well established. The 1891 census of Ireland showed there to be a "labour aristocracy, in Ulster, definable in terms of religion",[47] whereas in Belfast, the industrial capital of Ireland, industry was dominated by unionists who saw it to be within their financial interests to stay within the empire. Catholics at the time accounted for 5,008 of the 8,900 people in Ulster workhouses that year, a rate of 55% while the Catholic population of the province was 46%. By 1901, Belfast Catholics were "underrepresented in the professions, such as accountancy, and in middle-class employment, such as in insurance and banks" and were "underrepresented in the skilled working class jobs and

---

46   McVeigh and Rolston, p. 210.
47   Geoffrey Bell. 1976. *The Protestants of Ulster.* 3rd ed. London: Pluto Press, p. 19.

overrepresented in domestic service".[48] As Geoffrey Bell points out in the 1901 census:

> There is an interesting contrast between employment in the civil service and local government. Male Catholic workers in the civil service were actually overrepresented while in local government the reverse applied, suggesting that discrimination did not apply where the central Westminster government exercised control but that where the local unionists did, Catholics were at a marked disadvantage.[49]

While Bell might be being kind in excusing the Westminster government's role in propagating and empowering the unionist ideology that abused its power in such a fashion, it does not alter his observation that Westminster and the local unionists have differed in their approaches to the North since partition. British imperial policy, up to the present day, by virtue of the Good Friday Agreement and associated subsequent agreements, prefers the integration of a core of the other into the colonial project in order to quell dissent. In handing over the reins of the Northern state to unionists, while undoubtedly cognisant of how the unionists operated, upon partition they laid the foundation for the abuses that would follow. The new Northern state structure "marked

---

48 Bell, p. 21.
49 Ibid.

a volte face in British imperial policy". "Instead of the native incorporation that had been progressing since the Act of Union [1800], Northern Ireland reverted to settler 'responsibility' mode,"[50] and "permanent vigilance became the motto of the new regime"[51] as James Craig set about creating "a new impregnable Pale".[52]

In 1934, though the system had been running already for 13 years, James Craig confirmed the vision for the Northern state when he told the Northern House of Commons: "It is undoubtedly our duty and our privilege, and always will be, to see that those appointed by us possess the most unimpeachable loyalty to the King and Constitution. That is my whole object in carrying on a Protestant government for a Protestant people."[53] Craig got his wish. Domination was ensured at the polls with the postponement of the 1923 local elections until 1924, the abandonment of proportional representation (STV) voting in favour of first past the post, and the reorganisation of electoral boundary lines, meaning that where nationalists had controlled 25 of almost 80 local councils in 1920 that number had fallen to two in 1924.[54]

---

50    McVeigh and Rolston, p. 208.
51    Brendan O'Leary. 2019. *A treatise on Northern Ireland, Volume II: Control*. Oxford: Oxford University Press, p. 18.
52    Cornelius O'Leary and Patrick Maume. 2004. *Controversial Issues in Anglo-Irish Relations 1910–1921*. Dublin: Four Courts Press, p 146-156.
53    Northern Ireland House of Commons. Parliamentary Debates, Volume XVII. Columns 72-73.
54    Brendan O'Leary, Volume II, p. 41.

A class-based franchise was also enforced, with the ruling UUP deciding that the benefits of disenfranchising working class Catholics would outweigh the disenfranchisement of working class Protestants. Voting rights would extend to local government taxpayers and their spouses, as well as company votes, which gave directors of a company up to six votes depending on their company's contribution to local tax, granting these directors more than one vote each, assuming that they were property owners and thus local ratepayers. This "legal framework enabled unionists to win 'majority' control where there were demographic nationalist majorities – for example, in Omagh, Derry, Armagh, and Fermanagh".[55] In 1946, as Clement Atlee was setting about reforming the franchise in Britain, the UUP was working to restrict it further in the North, with the Representation of the People Act removing the franchise from lodgers who were not ratepayers themselves.[56] Lancelot Curran, the UUP Chief Whip, declared such measures necessary because "the best way to prevent the overthrow of the government by people who had no stake in the country and had not the welfare of the people of Ulster at heart was to disenfranchise them".[57] Brendan O'Leary estimates that estimates that the "UUP's excess of seats in nine out of ten elections after 1929 was over

---

55 Ibid., p. 43.
56 Ibid.
57 Michael Farrell. 1976. *Northern Ireland: The Orange State*. London: Pluto Press, p. 85-86.

10%",[58] creating a system whereby "incentives to participate for republicans or socialists among the nationalist population were also radically reduced",[59] as is perhaps best seen in the complaints of the nationalist leader Joseph Devlin: "We have no place in the administration of the province whose laws we are supposed to accept, and do accept. I do not think the representations we make have the slightest possible effect."[60]

Disenfranchised politically, Catholics also felt the brunt of the new Northern state materially: by 1927 and 1937, the wards in Belfast with the most Catholics were the ones with the worst housing conditions.[61] Despite there being more Catholics aged between 0-14 in the Falls Road area in 1937 than Protestants on the Shankill, by 1971[62] no such majority was visible in the over 30 age groupings, showing that Catholics had been forced to move elsewhere to seek work that was not in their hometown. The labour aristocracy had continued as well, with Bell noting that the 1971 census showed that "apart from the small Court ward, the three areas with the highest unemployment [in Belfast] are the areas with the highest proportion of Catholics", and "the area with the highest proportion of managerial and self-employed (with staff) has the lowest number of Catholics"[63] and the 1975 work of

---

58    O'Leary, Volume II, p. 48.
59    Ibid.
60    Farrell, p. 149.
61    Bell, p. 25.
62    Ibid., p. 27.
63    Ibid.

Edmund A. Aunger stating that that Protestant males were typically skilled workers and Catholic males were typically unskilled workers.[64] The unionist Shankill was found to have double the proportion of men in foremen jobs compared to republican Falls, double the number of cars, half the amount unemployed, and double the amount of owner-occupiers. Catholics had a far lower proportion of middle class and upper working class jobs and worse housing conditions. Writing in 1976, Bell said: "Protestant privileges remain at all class levels."[65] Patterns like this repeated themselves in the areas of Armagh with the highest Catholic populations and in the majority-Catholic towns and cities of Newry, Strabane and Derry. Reflecting this was a much higher emigration rate among Catholics: between 1937 and 1971, the number of Catholics emigrating for every non-Catholic emigrating ranged from 2.3 to 2.8.[66]

If the oppressed Catholic workers in the new Northern state were hoping for some solidarity from their unionist counterparts, they were sorely mistaken. While there had been some hope that the working class of Belfast could join together in the early 20th century, this was largely dashed by the beginning of the Irish revolutionary period when the Protestant workers became unionist workers – deciding, in

---

64   Edmund A. Aunger. 1975. "Religion and Occupational Class in Northern Ireland," *Economic and Social Review*, Volume 7, Issue 1, p. 1-17.

65   Bell., p. 28.

66   Brendan O'Leary, Volume II, p. 51.

a process that involved the expulsion of so-called "rotten Prods", i.e., socialist Protestants, as their bosses had, that their financial interests were to be better taken care of under the yoke of the British empire. While there was brief hope of working class unity sparked by the 1932 Outdoor Relief riots, these were quickly scuppered again and unionist workers largely functioned as a disciplining force, only invoking their collective power when they deem the union with Britain to be under threat – the 1974 Ulster Workers' Council strike being the most prominent example of this, a two-week strike that brought down the power-sharing government that had been agreed under the Sunningdale Agreement. An arrangement not identical to, but not unlike, the power-sharing arrangement currently in place at Stormont.

Bell explains how labour was disciplined in the name of the union, and it is worth quoting him at length:

> As with so much the explanation in the end comes back to Ulster unionism. That the unionist alliance has been an all-class alliance, that through that alliance the Protestant workers have gained marginal privileges, that within the alliance the Orange Order, controlled by the unionist establishment, provides a social service for the Protestant worker – all this not only helps to prevent the emergence of class consciousness, it also provides an alternative for the services normally associated with trade unions: social life, a "brotherhood", a preservation

of a labour aristocracy. Like many other trade unionists, the Protestant trade unionists have been "bought off", not, however, through the normal channels of industrial disputes and compromises, but through a distinct political system; and their craft mentality is sustained, not so much through a form of trade unionism, but through a process of economic and social differentials which has its roots in that political system. And if, on occasions, economic agitation has threatened to disrupt the pattern, the threat has never been carried out. The unionist establishment has always neutralised it, as they did in 1932 by labelling it a Catholic plot and by promoting, nakedly, a policy of jobs for Protestants first.[67]

The unionist labour movement also played its part in the militarisation of the Northern state upon its foundation, which arose out of the Ulster Volunteer Force (UVF) paramilitary founded in 1912, coming after that was the Ulster Unionist Labour Association (UULA), which "provided the backbone to a vigilante group which acted in turn as a parasite militia in the run-up to the creation of the Northern Ireland state".[68] The UULA and UVF were eventually consolidated into the B

---

67  Bell, p. 88.
68  Stewart et al, p. 73.

Specials,[69] "Ulster's stormtroopers",[70] who carried out various pogroms against Catholics in every decade from the 1920s to the '60s. Security for the Northern state was "perpetuated by full-time and part-time employment for workers, mostly from the politically and demographically dominant Protestant community".[71] Catholic civilians made up the bulk of those killed during the violence of 1920-1922 in the North, with 266 killed as opposed to 179 Protestant civilians, 32 members of Crown Forces, and eight republicans.[72] Orange halls were used to recruit and distribute weaponry[73] as B Specials numbers grew to 19,000 by the summer of 1922, the force serving as a uniformed reserve for the A Specials[74] and contributing to a situation guaranteeing permanent vigilance, where one in five protestant males were members of the RUC.[75] An atmosphere was created where "only the most egregious and publicized of independent loyalist violent assaults on Catholics produced any disciplinary restraint on the part of the authorities",[76] and the usual killings, burnings out, and

---

69   Paul Bew, Peter Gibbon, and Henry Patterson. 2002. *Northern Ireland 1921/2001: Political Forces and Social Classes.* London: Serif, p. 18-19.

70   Peter O'Rourke. 3 February 2016. "The B-Specials – Unionism's stormtroopers". *An Phoblacht*.

71   Stewart et al, p. 73.
72   Brendan O'Leary, Volume II, p. 20.
73   Ibid., p. 22.
74   Ibid., p. 23.
75   Ibid., p. 24.
76   Ibid., p. 29.

intimidation central to pogroms – "now called sectarian or ethnic cleansing"[77] – proceeded with the approval of the new state.

A confluence of government, industry, and labour united upon the oppression of a designated other, constantly utilising their state-sanctioned paramilitaries to strike terror into the othered community; this is Fascism before, during, and after the reigns of Hitler and Mussolini.

To fully understand how unionism functioned during the span of the Orange state from 1921 until direct rule came into effect into 1972 is to understand a past that modern-day unionism harks back to fondly. With Catholics now integrated into most levels of Northern society and with its political power greatly shrunken by the power-sharing arrangements of the Good Friday Agreement, it finds itself left to focus on cultural issues such as the Irish language and the GAA, both of which it vehemently opposes at every turn, still wantonly displaying the mindset of the planter, portraying the native culture as something to be suppressed, distanced from, something of which the natives should be ashamed.

It is also to the benefit of middle-class republicans to not elucidate such criticisms of unionism. This subset of the middle class has always existed in one form or another, represented by the conservative Catholic, constitutionally

---

77   Ibid., p. 19.

nationalist SDLP, but has grown into itself in the peace process era; as Liam Ó Ruairc points out, the Executive Office's January 2018 Labour Force Survey Religion Report found that found while 76% of working-age Protestants and 66% of working-age Catholics were economically active in 1992, this had evened out to 75% and 74% respectively by 2016. The rates of economic inactivity had gone from 24% for Protestants and 34% for Catholics to 25% and 26%.[78] A 2003 study found that social mobility was greater among Catholics, with only 17% of Catholics who were within the highest social and economic category having been born in it, compared to 33% of Protestants.[79] While unionists talk of "losing out" under the peace process, the stats clearly tell the story of an evening out of the share of the economy. With the paternal British hand returned to activity within Northern politics by the direct rule era and then fully codified by the Good Friday Agreement, the imperial policy of integration has firmly returned. Integrated and fully cosseted, these middle- and upper-class republicans have no wish to interrogate the politics of those with whom Sinn Féin – the party they vote for in droves – shares power. If they did, they might ask why their ascension to equality is considered a loss for the other community and be exposed to the fascistic

---

78  Ó Ruairc, p. 102.
79  Richard Breen. 15 December 2003. "Social mobility and constitutional and political preferences in Northern Ireland". *The British Journal of Sociology*, Volume 52: Issue Four, p. 621-645.

belief that still determines unionism. For unionists, one might ask how they still have not come to the realisation that the integration of Catholics and so-called republicans into the British system works to strengthen the union. Therein lies the great contradiction within their ideology, one of local domination and colonial abdication. Their support for British control in Ireland is undermined by the British colonial policy of integration that they have implemented here and elsewhere. It is for these reasons that just about every crisis in unionist history, including the current one of the Protocol, centres around one question: which do they prefer, the maintenance of the union, or the domination over Catholics? The latter being the guarantor of the former means that they have no satisfactory answer.

The existence of the Northern state is a denial of democracy. The last time Ireland expressed its national will as a unified body politic was the 1918 general election, in which Sinn Féin won 73 seats, the Irish Unionist Alliance won 22, and the reformist constitutional nationalist Irish Parliamentary Party won six. The national aspiration was clearly one of independence and self-determination, an aspiration that was denied when Britain partitioned the country and created two new states, one of which was the Northern state, concentrated around the one small area with a unionist majority in Ireland, where the majority of the industry was also located. The Northern state originates in "the British state's refusal to recognise the right of the people of Ireland as a whole to self-determination".[80] Democracy is impossible within its constraints, meaning that any body or organisation that enters its institutions is bound to neglect democracy, as mainstream republicanism has done by signing up to the border poll mechanism contained within the Good Friday Agreement, which is now the only accepted mechanism by which partition can be ended. The border poll is formulated on partitionist principles, accepting the base idea that the will of the majority in the North partitioned Ireland and thus only the will of the majority in the North can end it. What this ignores, of course, is that "partition had created this majority in the first place, making it artificial".[81] The fact that a border poll can only be called by the British Secretary of State for the North, with no set criteria and no obligation on the secretary to specify such criteria, is just another contravention of democracy that has been signed up to; surely, self-determination only at the express permission of the colonial master is oxymoronic.

In entering the political institutions, Sinn Féin leave themselves open to criticism for administering British-enforced austerity and neglect in the economy while proclaiming to be a left-wing party and they often correctly rebut this criticism by pointing to the miserly amounts supplied in the block grant. The question for them, as a

---

80 Ó Ruairc, p. 7.
81 Ibid., p. 11.

supposed republican party, is why play the part when they can see the game is rigged? The question is the same for them when it comes to the political institutions: why celebrate that the 2022 election in the North made Michelle O'Neill the First Minister in waiting for a state that they want to abolish? Why show such interest in resurrecting the Northern institutions, as they have done, when they still ensure a unionist veto and deny Irish self-determination? Brendan Hughes, the former officer commanding of the Belfast Brigade of the IRA and the leader of the 1980 H-Block hunger strike, predicted the current impasse in 2001. "The sad thing about all this is that the British set this up," he said:

> This is the British answer to the republican problem in Ireland. It's a British solution, it's not an Irish solution. It's not a solution that we have control of. There are people up there and the British ministers are handing money out, but the whole thing is built on sand. First of all the statelet still exists. Secondly, whenever Tony Blair, or whoever comes after him, decides – or the Unionists decide – to walk out, the Good Friday Agreement is finished. It's all finished.[82]

Hughes' description that republicanism was powerless within

---

82 Brendan Hughes. 25 January 2001. "Brendan Hughes on the 20th Anniversary of the Hunger Strikes". *The Blanket: A Journal of Protest and Dissent*. Available at: https://theblanket.ulib.iupui.edu/BH30208.html [Accessed 14 October 2022].

the agreed mechanisms of the peace process era brings to mind the question asked by the veteran republican socialist Bernadette Devlin McAliskey: "What power and what sharing?"[83]

Now, after 25 years of participation in the British solution for republicanism, Sinn Féin are left holding the bag for Stormont as Hughes' prophecy comes true. While the flattening of the labour aristocracy and Sinn Féin's electoral success in 2022 may mark the symbolic end of republicans being denied a seat at the table, what has been forgotten is that Irish republicanism is about constructing Ireland's own table – not eating at Britain's. Beholden to a *modus operandi* formulated within the British-dictated terms of engagement, having neglected the development of republican political thought, Sinn Féin finds itself unable to articulate that the way out of this predictable predicament is the defeat of unionism, rather than collaboration with it in the halls of Stormont and the integration of it into its supposed "new and agreed Ireland", and building a political project outside of the accepted parameters of sharing power.

---

[83] 13 May 2016. "Bernadette Devlin McAliskey: What does she think of Stormont nearly 50 years on?". *Derry Journal*.

## 4. Cultural Neglect: No Moon

If there is one area in which the contemporary republican inability to conceive of politics outside of the British terms of engagement has been badly exposed, it is that of language policy. Although an Irish language act – known among activists as *Acht na Gaeilge* and now officially the Identity and Language (Northern Ireland) Act – was agreed in the 2006 St Andrews Agreement, resulting in the 2007 resurrection of the Stormont Assembly with the DUP and Sinn Féin at its head, the legislation to give the native Irish language official status within the Northern state as has been done with Welsh in Wales and Gàidhlig in Scotland was never put in place. When the DUP-Sinn Féin power-sharing Executive collapsed due to DUP leader and First Minister Arlene Foster's refusal to temporarily step aside amid an investigation into her role in the Renewable Heat Incentive scandal, Sinn Féin then made a renewed promise for the implementation of *Acht na Gaeilge* a condition for returning to Stormont. Thousands march yearly in protests known as *Lá Dearg* – Red Day, to go with the slogan *Dearg le Fearg* (red with anger) – in support of official recognition and the associated rights for the Irish language, and 2017 saw a crowd of 12,000 people.[1] Republican voters backed Sinn Féin's refusal to go back to Stormont with an *Acht*, and with momentum on their side it appeared that they would stand strong, until they agreed a deal in 2018 that would have returned the power-sharing Executive with no *Acht*. This was averted when the DUP, under pressure from unionist paramilitaries, collapsed the talks at the last minute.

The *New Decade, New Approach* deal that was eventually agreed to resurrect Stormont once again contained within it agreement to grant official status to the Irish language within the Northern state, to repeal a 1737 ban on the use of the language in the courts, to allow members of the Assembly to use the language for official business in Stormont, and to appoint an Irish language commissioner. Faced with continued unionist intransigence on the implementation of protection for the language in the summer of 2021, Sinn Féin did the only thing it could do within the framework it now operates: it ran to the British government – just as it did when unionists consistently blocked abortion and same-sex marriage legalisation – and had them agree to legislate for

---

1 Jane McAteer. 20 May 2017. "An Lá Dearg march draws big crowd for march through Belfast demanding Irish Language rights". [online] *An Dream Dearg*. Available online at: https://www.dearg.ie/en/nuacht/cartlann/030140-la-dearg-big-crowd [Accessed 16 October 2022].

an *Acht* over the head of Stormont,[2] once again invoking the Westminster policy of integration. Westminster set itself the deadline of October 2021 for the implementation of an *Acht*, a deadline that it missed. By the time Stormont had collapsed again in February 2022, no legislation on the language had been moved forward. Against a backdrop of as many as 17,000 people taking to the streets for Lá Dearg 2022,[3] *Acht na Gaeilge* was introduced in Westminster in May 2022 and received royal assent in December 2022. Its implementation will now depend on the functioning of Stormont.

The problem facing Sinn Féin and mainstream republicanism is that it is now exclusively confined to these halls of power, be they in Dublin, Belfast or London. The republicanism of the streets is now dead, and any demand that is taken to the streets such as the Lá Dearg protests are designated as targets by Sinn Féin to become yet another parliamentary demand in the name of delivering the stated goals of the peace process. Indeed, in 2011, Sinn Féin's then-Minister for Culture, Arts and Leisure Carál Ní Chuilín stated that she would introduce "measures aimed at depoliticising the Irish language and returning it to a status where it can

---

2  Mary Lou McDonald. 16 June 2021. "British government agree to legislate for *Acht Gaeilge* – McDonald". [online] *Sinn Féin*. Available at: https://www.sinnfein.ie/contents/61136 [Accessed on 16 October 2022].

3  Diarmuid Pepper. 21 May 2022. "Thousands take part in Belfast march in support of Irish Language Act". [online] *The Journal*. Available at: https://www.thejournal.ie/belfast-irish-language-act-an-dream-dearg-5770204-May2022/ [Accessed on 16 October 2022].

be practiced and enjoyed by people of all backgrounds and all traditions".[4] With this pronouncement, Ní Chuilín was displaying Sinn Féin's willingness to reform its own approach to the Irish language. Having previously been central to the radical approach to its spread in Belfast in the 1980s, the party has now taken on the Westminster approach to the language, which Feargal Mac Ionnrachtaigh, channelling the work of Patricia Kachuk, described as "attempting to incorporate the language into the discourse of the 'two traditions in Northern Ireland' by consciously isolating radical language initiatives."[5] The language activist Pádraig Ó Maolchraoibhe describes how the British government would "co-operate with 'respectable' Irish speakers in order to marginalise"[6] more radical elements of the movement to go about "taking the Irish language out of politics".[7] Since the devolution of powers following the Good Friday Agreement, the majority representatives of the republican/nationalist people – first the SDLP and then Sinn Féin – have taken up this strategy as a means of imposing consensus and disciplining the radical elements who stand outside of the Good Friday Agreement's consensus politics. In Belfast's Irish language community, this was perhaps best seen when *LÁ* Nua, the predecessor to Ireland's first ever Irish language daily newspaper, LÁ, was

---

4   6 September 2011. "PSNI officers sign up for Irish lessons". *The Irish News.*
5   Mac Ionnrachtaigh, p. 179.
6   Ibid., p. 183.
7   Ibid.

defunded by Foras na Gaeilge, the all-Ireland Irish language governing body that was founded by both governments in Ireland following the Good Friday Agreement, after it had given voice to people within the Irish language community who were critical of how the DUP-Sinn Féin duopoly had treated the language.[8]

In embracing parliamentarianism, Sinn Féin has fallen into the trap of thinking immediate delivery is all that matters. Allowing for and actively encouraging the occupying British government to legislate for the protection of our native language is just an outworking of this approach; where immediate delivery is all that matters, neither the method of delivery nor the content of what is delivered is of any importance and short-term policies are valued over tangible and material gains. Just as republican political thought and principles have been left to wither on the vine, so too have the traditional cultural demands of the movement – that of an Ireland *"Ní hamháin saor ach Gaelach, agus ní hamháin Gaelach ach saor comh maith"*, not just free but Gaelic, and not just Gaelic but free too.

It is a far cry from the words of Máirtín Ó Cadhain, the republican socialist, novelist and native Irish speaker interned in the Curragh camp during World War II, who said: *"Sí an Ghaeilge athghabháil na hÉireann agus is í athghabháil na*

---

8   17 December 2008. "LÁ Nua a victim of 'dispensation of power-sharing'". *Andersonstown News*.

*hÉireann slánú na Gaeilge"*; Irish is the reconquest of Ireland and the reconquest of Ireland is the salvation of Irish. The reconquest as a concept passed down from James Connolly to Ó Cadhain to republicans of the provisional movement such as Bobby Sands and Jim Lynagh, men who spent their time interned in the H-Blocks of Long Kesh reading Frantz Fanon, Che Guevara, Antonio Gramsci, and Ho-Chi Minh to develop their theories of a self-sufficient Ireland,[9] one that is, as Sands wrote, "free in mind and body, separate and distinct physically, culturally and economically".[10] The physical, cultural and economic all share equal footing in Sands' understanding of freedom; with the official standing of the Irish language now under the thumb of Westminster, however, the fear is that a sole focus on its legal status and its financial backing from the occupying state will mean that the cultural joins the economic and the physical in being unfree.

What is particularly frustrating about the neglect of Sands' conception of the combination of the political and the cultural as paths to freedom and self-sufficiency is that the Irish language, along with the Gaelic Athletic Association, is one of the strongest examples of self-sufficiency and

---

9    Dieter Reinisch. 6 August 2018. "Dreaming of an "Irish Tet Offensive": Irish Republican prisoners and the origins of the Peace Process". [online] *The Irish Story*. Available at: https://www.theirishstory.com/2018/08/06/dreaming-of-an-irish-tet-offensive-irish-republican-prisoners-and-the-origins-of-the-peace-process/#.Y0tOCuzMLEY [Accessed 16 October 2022].

10    Bobby Sands. 1997. *Writings from Prison*. Cork: Mercier Press, p. 314.

organising among Catholics in the North. In 1969, five families established what is known variously as *Gaeltacht Bóthar Seoighe, Pobal Feirste,* or the Irish Houses, a new development on west Belfast's Shaw's Road where Irish is the main language. The original five houses were built by hand by the small community that lived there, and over time the community stretched to 22 houses – houses which can only be bought by people who pledge to make Irish the first language of the home. Where *Gaeltacht Bóthar Seoighe's* main influence is felt is *gaelscolaíocht*, Irish language education, in the Northern state. These families established *Bunscoil Phobal Feirste* in 1971 to serve their children. It was the first *gaelscoil* – or *bunscoil* as they are known in the Northern state – in the North. Over 50 years later, there are over 7,000 children in *bunscoileanna* throughout the six counties, and there are two *gaelcholáiste* – second-level schools – too. This has led to a great growth in the prevalence of the native language: the 2021 census showed that 12.4% (228,600) of people aged three and over in the North had some ability in the language, an increase from 10.7% (184,900 people) in 2011.[11] *Bunscoil Phobal Feirste* received no official recognition from the North's Department of Education until 1985, by which time it was already a success. It, and other cultural endeavours focused on the language in Belfast's west such as *Cumann Chluain Ard*

---

11  Northern Ireland Statistics and Research Agency. 22 September 2022. *Main Statistic for Northern Ireland Statistical Bulletin – Language.* Belfast.

and *Cultúrlann McAdam Ó Fiaich*, are evidence of what can be created when a community builds itself, away from the auspices of the occupying state.

Sands espoused the idea of self-sufficient communities within the republican enclaves of the North, communities that disengaged from the occupying state and were self-policed, self-taught, self-organised and self-sufficient. Building on these ideas and the Maoist tracts he had read in prison, his IRA comrade Jim Lynagh developed an idea of an Irish People's War where the architecture of British occupation – RUC stations, British army installations etc. – would be removed by force in order to create the no-go zones that would make these kind of self-contained communities possible. Theirs is the road not taken, the ideology neglected and left to curdle as the peace process era further incorporates republicans while forcing them to leave their republicanism at the door. Yet Sinn Féin still commemorate Sands and Lynagh every year, songs referencing them such as "Roll of Honour" and "Loughgall Ambush" remain among the most popular of republican ballads. The men and their memories still exist in the mainstream republican imaginary, but they are decorative, only to be commemorated and never to have their ideas analysed or progressed. "A culture which takes place only in museums is already exhausted," Mark Fisher wrote. "A culture of commemoration is a cemetery. No cultural object can retain its power when there are no longer new eyes to see it."[12] Therein lies the great malaise and neglect of peace process era republicanism; new eyes are no longer tuned to ideas such as *athghabháil na hÉireann*; songs are sung of Sands and Lynagh and then modern republicans get back to promoting ideas that were antithetical to the republican movement when the two were alive. There is certainly a feeling within the Irish language community that the language movement has lost its radical edge, as is attested to by activists Eoghan Ó Néill[13] and Liam Ó Maolchluiche[14] who learned the language while imprisoned in Long Kesh – with Sands, among others – in the work of Mac Ionnrachtaigh.

The reclamation of the radical edge to the language movement lies in a return to its recent past, where the foundation of Gaeltacht Bóthar Seoighe was followed not long after by the beginning of bunscoileanna in the North. The movement, however, was not fully galvanised until the 1981 hunger strike and the death of the Irish-speaking Sands served as a cataclysmic rupture that re-energised political action in the republican community and "transformed the views of people who had never thought of the Irish language as a means of struggle before".[15] The Bóthar Seoighe founder Seamás Mac Seáin attests that the wider

---

12   Mark Fisher. 26 January 2007. "Coffee Bars and Internment Camps". *K-punk: The Collected and Unpublished Writings of Mark Fisher from 2004-2016*. London: Repeater Books, p. 182.

13   Mac Ionnrachtaigh, p. 210.

14   Ibid., p. 214.

15   Ibid., p. 157.

community had donated to Bóthar Seoighe financially, but they "had not played an active role in our project until after the hunger strike",[16] and the 1985 west Belfast survey work carried out by Féilim Ó hAdhmaill corroborates this version of events: 87% of those surveyed had decided to learn the language between 1981 and 1984 with 70% citing Bobby Sands and the H-Block protests as an influence in doing so.[17] To capitalise on this, Sinn Féin, in their long-shed revolutionary guise, founded the party's Roinn an Chultúir (Cultural Department) in 1982, which oversaw "scores of additional language classes"[18] that linked the language to the "history of colonialism in Ireland and the policies of the hostile British government accordingly".[19] Classes were held "where people were comfortable, whether it be in their own living room or the local community centre",[20] ensuring that the language was brought to the people. This approach to the spread of the Irish language took on a bottom-up shape thanks to its "language-learning model of informal education, which saw the 'pupil' become the 'teacher' after arriving at a particular level of fluency".[21] Parents who could not speak the language but sent to their children to local

---

16   Ibid., p. 158.
17   Feilim Ó hAdhmaill. 1985. *Report of a Survey Carried out on the Irish Language in West Belfast*. Belfast: Glór na nGael
18   Mac Ionnrachtaigh, p. 160.
19   Ibid., p. 162.
20   Ibid., p. 161.
21   Ibid., p. 192.

bunscoileanna were encouraged to take up lessons, with one bunscoil in Ballymurphy making it compulsory that at least one parent would take up the learning of the language,[22] thereby ensuring the involvement of the community in what Roinn an Chultúir founder Terry Enright called "a liberating education amongst ordinary people".[23]

What this monumental effort demonstrated was what James Connolly called "a policy of self-reliance, and confident trust in a people's own power of self-emancipation by a people",[24] and turned Enright's "ordinary people" into Paulo Freire's "responsible subjects" whose development of critical consciousness "leads the way to the expression of social discontents precisely because these discontents are real components of an oppressive situation".[25] This education allowed the republican people of the North to experience what Helen Ó Murchú called a "liberation from the understanding that they are dependent, that things happen to them, that they have control over their own cultural future".[26] Previous to the foundation of Gaeltacht Bóthar Seoighe, attempts were made by the group Fal to found an

---

22   Ibid., p. 175.
23   Ibid., p. 161.
24   Connolly, Sinn Féin and the Language Movement
25   Introduction of Donaldo Macedo in: Paulo Freire. 2005. *Pedagogy of the Oppressed: 30th Anniversary Edition*. New York: Continuum, p. 36.
26   John Walsh. 2011. *Contests and Contexts: The Irish language and Ireland's socio-economic development*. Bern: Peter Lang, p. 98.

Irish-language shop and credit union in Belfast in the 1950s,[27] and while these attempts failed, they too showed the spirit of what Mac Ionnrachtaigh calls "acting decisively"[28] and what Fran Lisa Buntman calls "social creativity": "introducing new values and aims, new forms of co-operation and action".[29] The key to ceasing republicanism's descent into a culture of commemoration is in the reclamation of the decisive action of the 80s, when political ferment was matched with cultural revolution, an elucidation of how Irish life could be lived away from the yoke of the British state. This history is barely history, beginning in earnest with the foundation of Gaeltacht Bóthar Seoighe in 1969, meaning that our responsible subjects are, for the most part, still with us, and the spirit of volunteerism is by no means dead, with Mac Ionnrachtaigh noting that "the establishment, development and long-term sustainability of Irish-medium schools still largely depend on bottom-up voluntary endeavour".[30] If the Irish language is to be truly saved as a means of communication in the North then it will be "best served by that politics which does not necessarily applaud for its symbolic role as the main vehicle for Irish identity but rather creates the environment for it to

---

27  Vincent Mc Kee. 1997. *Gaelic Nations: Politics of the Gaelic language in Scotland and Northern Ireland in the 20th Century.* London: The Bluestack Press, p. 28-29.

28  Mac Ionnrachtaigh, p. 175.

29  Fran Lisa Buntman. 2003. *Robben Island and Prisoner Resistance to Apartheid.* Cambridge: Cambridge University Press, p. 236.

30  Mac Ionnrachtaigh, p. 209.

grow and develop".[31] This environment will not be found in Stormont legislation, but rather in the duplication of the Bóthar Seoighe project in other areas of Belfast, Derry City, Strabane, Newry, etc., in the foundation of economic interests titled towards the language such as Fal's credit union, in the return of language classes to a bottom-up and anywhere, everywhere model, and in the facilitation of cultural life through Irish, to which Belfast's all-Irish GAA club Laochra Loch Lao and institutions such as Cultúrlann and Cumann Chluain Ard remain positive examples.

In such examples and ideas lies the genesis of a strategy of withdrawal, whereby the continuing failure to operate the institutions of the Northern state are taken as the political catalyst to create a new form of life away from the auspices of the state – just as the hunger strikes proved. Only in alliance with the radicalised republican trade unions could this strategy possibly be a success, creating a situation where the republican community could bring the Northern state to a standstill via strikes and public disobedience. Lá Dearg, for all its worth, could not be said to be confrontational or bringing the state to a standstill, as the weekend marches proceed along routes agreed with the PSNI and other authorities. This strategy of withdrawal would bring the theories of Sands, Lynagh and Ó Cadhain into the present day and adapt them

---

31   Caoimhghin Ó Croidheáin. 2006. *Language from Below: The Irish language, ideology and power in 20<sup>th</sup> Century Ireland*. Bern: Peter Lang, p. 309.

for the current period of peacetime. If a newly energised republican movement were to decide to pursue the Éire Nua path as envisaged by Ó Brádaigh, or something similar, this would provide an ample opportunity to begin in a bottom-up approach with the community councils envisaged within the plan. Such organisation could serve as the beginning of the "thoroughgoing decolonisation envisaged by [Albert] Memmi or Ó Cadhain"[32] and the construction of a "truly decolonised identity".[33]

"Fascism attempts to organise the newly created proletarian masses without affecting the property structure which the masses strive to eliminate," wrote Walter Benjamin. "Fascism sees its salvation in giving these masses not their right, but instead a chance to express themselves. The masses have a right to change property relations; Fascism seeks to give them an expression while preserving property. The logical result of Fascism is the introduction of aesthetics into political life."[34] This process of aestheticisation necessarily creates what Kwame Nkrumah described as localised "instruments of

---

32 Tomás Mac Síomóin. 1994 "The Colonised Mind: Irish Language and Society" in *Reconsideration of Irish History and Culture: Selected Papers form the Desmond Greaves Summer School*, edited by Daltún Ó Ceallaigh. Dublin: Léirmheas, p. 69.
33 Ibid.
34 Walter Benjamin. 1935. "The Work of Art in the Age of Mechanical Reproduction". *Illuminations*. New York: Schocken Books, p. 241.

suppression on behalf of the neo-colonialists",[35] who prove correct Caoimhghin Ó Croidheáin's assertion that "national cultures are taken up by elites who wish to protect their political and economic interests".[36] This has then become the dominant cultural logic of the neoliberal age: a focus on the integration of various identities and cultures is created to satiate the alienation of colonised or oppressed peoples without ever addressing the historical displacement and dispossession that the people from these cultures experienced. That Sinn Féin would fall into this trap – a trap unionists are too blinded by their own inflexibility to see but one that Westminster has been setting around the world for centuries – shows the limits in the path that they have chosen, which has strayed into terrain that is a far cry from the ideologies of the martyrs they still hold as their spiritual forebears – Sands especially. Instead they appear doomed to follow the folly of the Irish Free State, where the "desire for genuine social change behind the revolutionary movement was diverted from social and political change in the form of Gaelicisation policies",[37] these being the placing of the language on street signs and the adoption of *Acht na Gaeilge* in the case of the Northern state. Perhaps these symbolic and safe gestures are simply a means of securing themselves against criticism

---

35 Kwame Nkrumah. 1964. *Consciencism: Philosophy and Ideology for Decolonisation and Development with Particular Reference to the African Revolution*. London: Panaf, p. 101.

36 Ó Croidheáin, p. 75.

37 Ibid., p. 170.

around the language as Sinn Féin prove that they will repeat the path of Fianna Fáil in the South before them and embrace Ireland's role as a comprador economy for Britain, the United States, and Europe. Ó Croidheáin writes that it is "no coincidence that elite interest in the Irish language went into terminal decline as the Irish Government established a new policy to attract foreign capital and multinational companies from the 1960s to the present day";[38] as Sinn Féin makes its peace with these elements, *Acht na Gaeilge* might be seen as its attempt at a farewell effort.

If Fascism seeks the aestheticisation of political life in order to maintain capitalism's property relations, it is thus the responsibility of any revolutionary movement tackling imperialism to do so by heeding the words of Edward Said and taking on the responsibility to "reclaim, rename and reinhabit the land",[39] and to create a "counter-hegemonic 'education for emancipation'" that retains power in the community and offers a "cultural and linguistic alternative to the dominant social model".[40] The "assertion of language rights by individuals and communities plays an important part in the revolutionary process of changing the general relations of power in Irish society",[41] but this is not enough, and "community-based organisations cannot afford to reduce

---

38 Ibid., p. 285.
39 Edward Said. 1993. *Culture and Imperialism*. London: Chatto & WIndus, p. 273.
40 Mac Ionnrachtaigh, p. 205.
41 Ó Croidheáin, p. 18.

their activism, to issue-based campaigns but must examine wider issues of land ownership, distribution of wealth and access to economic and political resources".[42] Even those in support of Sinn Féin's language policy could not pretend that it addresses such issues, and their actions in taking their concerns of An Dream Dearg to Westminster now means that the language risks "assimilation by the state and a reduction in their political effectiveness and a diminution of their social objectives".[43] We in Ireland have seen our language subsumed into the legislation of a counterrevolutionary state before following the foundation of the Irish Free State, and we have seen the damage that the depoliticisation that follows a failed phase of revolution can bring in terms of language activism: membership of Conradh na Gaeilge, the organisation founded in 1892 as part of the Gaelic Revival, for example, dropped from 700 branches in 1920 to 565 branches in 1922 – a figure that may exaggerate the number that were organised and active, given only 293 sent returns to an organisation-wide census.[44] Activists organising around language are thus better off on the outside of the state system, organising themselves, and "exerting pressure for a reconsideration and change of the accepted norms of society in terms of how society is structured and for whom it is organised".[45]

---

42   Ibid., p. 26.
43   Ibid.
44   Pádraig Ó Fearaíl. 1975. *The Story of Conradh na Gaeilge.* Dublin: Conradh na Gaeilge, p. 45.
45   Ó Croidheáin, p. 308.

The idea of an *Acht* from Westminster flies directly in the face of Sands' idea of an Ireland separate and free, economically, politically and culturally. As his sister, Bernadette Sands, said in 1998, Sands "did not die for nationalists to be equal British citizens within the Northern Ireland state".[46] A trap has been set, and whether it has been entered into purposefully is for the reader's interpretation, but it finds itself in the position that Connolly diagnosed as the death of any political movement: "The moment any organisation ceases to believe in the sufficiency of its own powers, the moment its membership begin to put their trust in powers not their own, in that moment that party or that organisation enters its decline."[47] Snookered politically, mainstream republicanism now tells us that the path to a united Ireland is to have the culture that Britain sought to destroy instead respected by them and its Irish proxies within a state whose very existence guarantees that there will be no united Ireland. The last extract of Sands' diary before his death on hunger strike in 1981 says that upon national freedom, the Irish will see "the rising of the moon". On the path that is currently being tread, there is no freedom – national, cultural, political, or economic – and there is no moon rising in sight.

---

46   1 February 1998. "Interview with Bernadette Sands". *Magill Magazine*.
47   Connolly, Sinn Féin and the Language Movement.

## 5. Conclusion: Revolutionary Neglect

What Britain does in Ireland via its economic control of the Northern state is to guarantee both dysfunction and poverty, but this is the point of the current arrangements of power. Power-sharing, when functioning, leaves republicans and unionists compromising for crumbs that would guarantee levels of neglect even if there were no ideological obstacles for either side to overcome. That neglect takes the form of the crippling levels of underfunding for key governance sectors, creating an economy beholden to private interests that fill the void and depress wages. It also guarantees poverty: 18% of the North lives in poverty, a rate that is especially felt among the children of the North, 24% of whom live in poverty.[1]

To attribute these conditions to British neglect would appear as a unionist position, supposing that Britain is failing in some paternalistic duty to the people of Ireland; the opposite

---

1   Chris Birt, Ben Drake, Carla Cebula, Aleks Collingwood, Joseph Elliott, David Leese, Peter Matejic, Gemma Schwendel, and Andrew Wenham. 16 March 2022. *Poverty in Northern Ireland 2022*. Joseph Rowntree Foundation.

is the case. This is what Britain wants. The low cost of living and wages guarantee cheap labour for their private enterprise and the power-sharing arrangement allows them to shield themselves from any blame for the governmental failures that are caused by their economic and political dominance. The current British approach to the North can be described as *give them enough rope*. It allows the British to point to the failures of devolution to Stormont and to say: if the Irish cannot work together at that level, how could they be trusted with an independent state whereby they are also expected to work with the South in a hypothetical united Ireland? The main thrust of Britain's argument in favour of retaining its colonial hold over Ireland has always been some variation on the idea that the Irish are not fit to govern themselves; through their funding that guarantees permanent austerity, they aim to prove the maxim.

That democracy is neglected is to Britain's satisfaction and by their design. In the most basic of senses, the power-sharing agreed to under the Good Friday Agreement means that if one political party miraculously collected 99% of the vote in the North, it still would not be entitled to govern alone. The absence of democracy in a state that was founded through the permanent circumnavigation of Irish democracy achieved by the partition of the nation is, of course, of no surprise. This neglect of democracy was then codified when the last of the opponents, the republicans, agreed to the partitionist arrangement of two border polls in the country should a border poll ever be called. The fact that such a hypothetical border poll is entirely within the gift of the Secretary of State and the Secretary of State alone is further evidence that there is no democracy to be had in the North and no self-determination in Ireland; it is Britain that remains the master of the country's destiny.

We cannot expect any opposition to these arrangements from the unionist parties. Theirs is an ideology of abdication, that believes in deference to Britain in all matters except for the domination of the Catholics. With Catholics no longer in the minority and now firmly enfranchised within the Northern state in the peace process era, this domination has become more difficult and, unable to conceive of how to take on such domination, they have simply taken their ball and gone home – refusing to engage in the very institutions designed to administer their *raison d'être*: the maintenance of the union. The Protocol presents a perfect opportunity for another episode of what Brendan O'Leary has termed "settler defiance of the metropolitan will",[2] as the unionists aim to maintain old structures in a changing Ireland. That this comes in the peace process era, when almost all of their demands have been met – when republicans have recognised and entered the Northern state institutions, the South has dropped its constitutional claim to the six counties

---

2   Brendan O'Leary, Volume II, p. 39.

of the North, the IRA has disarmed, forsworn the use of future political violence, and decommissioned all its arms – shows that the unionist ideology is primarily concerned with the presence of a neck under its boot rather than the achievement of concrete goals. Tony Blair famously stated in 1999 that unionists were "too stupid to realise that they have won".[3] What Blair didn't understand, or perhaps didn't want to admit, is that, to unionism, a victory that no longer enables them to wield the iron fist of industry and state-sponsored paramilitaries to crush the Catholics is a hollow one at best.

Nothing to halt this neglect can be expected of so-called neutral parties such as the Alliance Party. These "constitutional cowards"[4] attempt to obscure the focus on the national question via an insistence on addressing on-the-ground issues such as health first, never once reflecting on how the union is the guarantor of the neglect within those areas and that Ireland's lack of self-determination extends to the infrastructure of the North. Founded from the ashes of the unionist New Ulster Movement, these socially liberal centrists profess their interests to be making Stormont, and thus the Northern state, "work",[5] an unquestionably unionist

---

3   Alastair Campbell. 2012. *Diaries, Volume Three: Power and Responsibility*. London: Arrow Books, p. 66.

4   Brett Campbell. 28 September 2022. "Ireland's Future: Arlene Foster defends Alliance Party after SDLP accused them of being 'constitutional cowards' over rejection of event invite". *Belfast Telegraph*.

5   6 May 2022. "Naomi Long 'serious' about making Stormont work". [online] BBC News. Available at: https://www.bbc.co.uk/news/av/uk-northern-ireland-61352667 [Accessed 20 October 2022].

goal in the retention of the status quo, which is the union. It is because of their commitment to the status quo that the Alliance are trumpeted in some quarters, not least the South, as the saviours of the North as they have become the preferred vote of the liberal unionists, riding the wave of that constituency to come third in the two-horse race of the 2022 election. This is what makes the Alliance particularly pointless and rudderless; even when they do perform well electorally, their designation in the Stormont system as "other" rather than unionist means that they will never hold either of the top spots in the Executive, even if they receive 100% of the vote. One wonders why they go through the effort when there can be no reward given that their position could not be more clearly unionist. They vote to fund British Armed Forces Day in local councils, they refused to attend the Ireland's Future conference on possible new constitutional futures, multiple members and former members have complained that those in favour of a united Ireland within the party have been sidelined, and they reject calls for a border poll. The work of the University of Liverpool showed that 58.8% of Alliance voters in 2019 favoured the maintenance of the union, while only 25.6% favoured a united Ireland;[6] one gathers that the balance is even further to the side of unionism among their elected representatives.

So it falls to republicanism, which is, perhaps, why Sinn

---

6   Peter Shirlow and Jon Tonge. 2019. *University of Liverpool NI General Election Survey 2019*. University of Liverpool.

Féin have come in for the harshest criticism in this essay. Republicanism is Ireland's liberation ideology, meaning that those who claim it should be held to the highest of standards and critiqued or praised on the basis of their efforts to construct an Ireland that is independent in mind, body, and spirit as Bobby Sands envisioned. To do this, an alternative vision outside of the British-dictated rules of engagement must be envisioned and built, as it was in the lead-up to the Easter Rising of 1916 when organisations such as the GAA and *Conradh na Gaeilge* promoted an Irish cultural life, the Irish National Land League struck to abolish landlordism and fight for tenant farmers, Pádraig Pearse founded his school – *Scoil Éanna* – to deliver an Irish education, and James Connolly and Jim Larkin's Irish Transport and General Workers Union organised a working class that understood that its interests stretched beyond today's basic trade union demands of decent pay and extended to self-determination and democracy.

Frustration with Sinn Féin's abandonment of the Sands vision is especially acute when it is remembered that the party's electoral turn was begun by Sands's sacrifice. It was his election as an MP during the 1981 hunger strike that eventually claimed his life that led the party down the electoral path it now treads. At the 1981 party *ard fheis*, Danny Morrison, one of the foremost men behind the party's electoral turn, famously asked: "Who here really believes we can win the war through the ballot box? But will anyone here object if, with a ballot paper in one hand and an Armalite in this hand, we take power in Ireland?" The issue that has arisen is that in putting down the Armalite, as it always would eventually have to when it picked up the ballot box, Sinn Féin has grasped the ballot box with both hands rather than picking up a book, or a shovel, or anything else that would aid the building of an Irish revolutionary way of life. The party appears ready to take power in Ireland, in both the Northern and Southern states, as Morrison wanted, but the road from 1981 has seen them abandon almost every principle that they held, and if your passage through the halls of power requires the denunciation of principles and the signing over of control of Ireland's future to Britain, then who is really in power?

There is no *Acht na Gaeilge* that Westminster can deliver that will make up for what has been done to the Irish language by British colonialism for hundreds of years, just as there is no chance of any working class unity while working class unionists remain convinced that the maintenance of a union that guarantees that power remains offshore is in their best interests. The only accepted route towards ending this is now a border poll that can only be called by the British government and the question must be asked: if some version of republicanism is one day acceptable enough to the British government that they feel comfortable taking the chance of losing a border poll, is that republicanism truly a break from British domination? The history of the Republic, formerly

## Conclusion

the Irish Free State, testifies to the answer being no.

Therein lies the issue for Sinn Féin and the neglect that most urgently needs addressing in the North. The neglect of people, infrastructure, economy, and culture that happens in the Northern state is a fact of life under British colonialism, inescapable unless the colonial power is escaped. The Republic shows that nominal independence does not guarantee an end to this neglect and that a state founded on compromise of revolutionary values only serves to further the neglect if anything.

For republicanism, as Ireland's revolutionary tradition, Ruairí Ó Brádaigh's words ring as true as ever: sitting in Leinster House in Dublin is not a revolutionary activity, neither is sitting in Stormont in Belfast. The North has always suffered from a neglect of some sort, the British have ensured that, but the neglect it now suffers from is a neglect of our own making. The Armalite has been removed from the equation without being replaced as republicanism is confined to the halls of power in Dublin, London, and Belfast. What the North now suffers from most is the neglect of revolutionary activity.

www.ingramcontent.com/pod-product-compliance
Lightning Source LLC
Chambersburg PA
CBHW010032040426
42333CB00048B/2950